SPOTLIGHT

PRINCE EDWARD ISLAND

ANDREW HEMPSTEAD

Contents

PRINCE EDWARD ISLAND

CHARLOTTETOWN AND QUEENS COUNTY

As Atlantic Canada's smallest capital, Charlottetown (pop. 32,000)—the island's governmental, economical, cultural, and shopping center—makes no pretense of being a big city. Rather, this attractive town is walkable, comfortable, and friendly. Its major attractions include a beautiful harborside location, handsome public and residential architecture, sophisticated art and cultural happenings, and plentiful lodgings and appealing restaurants.

The city also makes a good sightseeing base for exploring surrounding Queens County, which is the definitive Prince Edward Island as you imagined the province would be. The region is temptingly photogenic, a meld of small seaports with brightly colored craft at anchor and farmland settings with limpid ponds and weathered barns. Along the Gulf of St. Lawrence is Cavendish, the island's most popular tourist destination. Cavendish was the childhood home of Lucy Maud Montgomery, who created perfection on earth within the pages of her books, which centered on the spunky heroine Anne of Green Gables.

PLANNING YOUR TIME

For many visitors, Queens County *is* Prince Edward Island. A typical itinerary may be that they catch the ferry to Wood Islands, spend one day in the capital, Charlottetown, and another in Cavendish before driving off the island via the Confederation Bridge. This is enough time in the capital to visit major attractions such as **Founders' Hall** and **Province House** while having enough time

© ANDREW HEMPSTEAD

HIGHLIGHTS

◖ Founders' Hall: Canadians especially will enjoy learning about how the Dominion of Canada was created at this harborfront interpretive center (page 13).

◖ Province House: This historic sandstone building in the heart of Charlottetown hosted the Fathers of Confederation in 1864 and continues today as the provincial seat of government (page 14).

◖ Victoria Park: Take a break from history with a walk through this waterfront park (page 15).

◖ International Shellfish Festival: You can feast on seafood year-round in Charlottetown, but this late-September festival is the place to try all your favorites at once (page 19).

◖ Confederation Players: Performers dressed in period costume lead small groups of interested visitors through the streets of historic downtown Charlottetown (page 24).

◖ Prince Edward Island National Park: Stretching along the Gulf of St. Lawrence, this park is one of the island's few undeveloped tracts of land. Warm water, beaches and dunes, and red cliffs are the main draws (page 28).

◖ North Rustico Harbour: It's just a dot on the map, but this small fishing village is particularly photogenic. A lighthouse, kayak tours, and an excellent restaurant add to the appeal (page 30).

◖ Green Gables House: Northern Queens County is lovingly known as "Anne's Land," for Anne of Green Gables, one of the world's best-known literary characters (page 32).

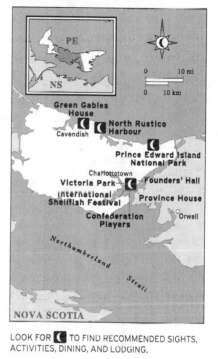

LOOK FOR ◖ TO FIND RECOMMENDED SIGHTS, ACTIVITIES, DINING, AND LODGING.

to join a **Confederation Players** tour and end the day with an evening walk through **Victoria Park.** If your travels coincide with the late September **International Shellfish Festival,** you may want to stay longer.

Cavendish, the most popular destination on all of Prince Edward Island, is just an hour's drive from the capital. This makes a day trip possible and means you can settle yourself into Charlottetown for two or more nights, taking advantage of the theater and many restaurants.

Cavendish does have many accommodations, but good dining rooms are severely lacking. Regardless of where you stay, your trip to Cavendish should include a drive through **Prince Edward Island National Park,** the short detour to **North Rustico Harbour,** and a visit to **Green Gables House.**

HISTORY

In 1755, England deported the Acadians from Acadia (Prince Edward Island, Nova Scotia,

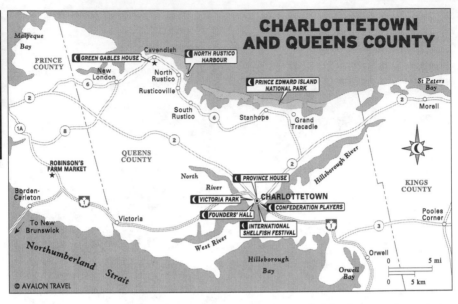

and New Brunswick) and swept the area again for Acadians in 1758. The English renamed the French fort at Port-la-Joye Fort Amherst and fortified the site. The English Crown dispatched surveyor Samuel Holland to survey, parcel out, and name various places and sites on the newly acquired island. Holland drew county lines on perplexing slants, dividing the island into 67 parcels, which were sold to absentee landlords at a lottery in England. Deciding Fort Amherst was difficult to defend, Holland moved the settlement across to the inner peninsula tip within Hillsborough Bay. He named it Charlotte, for the consort of King George III. The town's grid was laid out in 1764 and was named the island's capital the next year. During the American Revolution, American privateers sacked the capital, then added insult to injury when they stole the island's government seal and kidnapped the colonial governor.

Charlottetown has always been the island's main market town; the land now occupied by Province House and Confederation Centre was once the colony's thriving marketplace.

As in most early island towns, the majority of buildings were constructed of wood rather than stone, and many were subsequently leveled by fire. The stone buildings, however, survived. One of these is the small brick building at 104 Water Street—one of the capital's oldest buildings.

Growth

Charlottetown's development paralleled the island's development. A road network was laid out by 1850. And by 1860, some 176 sawmills were transforming forests into lumber, greasing the island's economy and providing the raw materials for a thriving shipbuilding industry. As the center of government and commerce, the town was enriched with splendid stone churches and public buildings. The building of St. Peter's Anglican Church at Rochford Square transformed a bog into one of the capital's finest areas in 1869. Beaconsfield, a tribute of Second Empire and Victorian gingerbread style at Kent and West Streets, was designed by architect William Critchlow Harris for wealthy shipbuilder

GETTING TO PRINCE EDWARD ISLAND

Most visitors to Prince Edward Island arrive by road, traveling either across the Confederation Bridge or on the ferry. You can also fly to Charlottetown.

CONFEDERATION BRIDGE

The impressive Confederation Bridge (902/437-7300 or 888/437-6565, www .confederationbridge.com) is Prince Edward Island's most important transportation link to the rest of Canada. From Cape Jourimain (New Brunswick), 80 kilometers east of Moncton, the bridge stretches across Northumberland Strait to Borden-Carlton, which is in Prince County, 60 kilometers west of Charlottetown. Driving across the impressive 12.9-kilometer span takes around 10 minutes (views are blocked by concrete barriers erected as a windbreak).

The round-trip bridge toll is $41.50 per vehicle including passengers. Payment (credit card, debit card, or cash) is collected at Borden-Carlton upon leaving the island.

BY FERRY

Prince Edward Island is also linked to the rest of Atlantic Canada by ferry. The mainland departure point is Caribou (Nova Scotia), near Pictou, a two-hour drive from Halifax. The ferry docks at Wood Islands, a scenic 62-kilometer drive southeast from Charlottetown. The 75-minute crossing is operated by **Northumberland Ferries** (902/566-3838 or 800/565-0201, www .peiferry.com) May to mid-December, with up to nine crossings in each direction daily during peak summer season. The round-trip fare is $61 per vehicle, regardless of the number of passengers. As with the bridge crossing, payment is made upon leaving the island. Therefore, take the ferry to PEI and return on the Confederation Bridge to save a few bucks.

BY AIR

Air Canada (888/247-2262, www.aircanada .com) has direct flights to Charlottetown from Halifax, Montréal, Ottawa, and Toronto. **WestJet** (403/250-5839 or 888/937-8538, www .westjet.com) flies in from Toronto.

and merchant James Peake in 1877. The Kirk of St. James was architect James Stirling's tribute to early Gothic Revival. The brick Charlottetown City Hall, at Queen and Kent Streets, was a local adaptation of Romanesque Revival. While the downtown precinct remains a hotbed of historical buildings, there is one exception. The confederation centennial prompted the federal government to mark the event by establishing the Confederation Centre of the Arts in Charlottetown in 1964, and the new complex became PEI's proud showplace for theater, art exhibits, and other presentations.

Sights and Recreation

Downtown Charlottetown is compact; plan on parking and exploring on foot. The waterfront area is the best place to leave your vehicle. Not only is it central, but you can make the harborside **Visitor Information Centre** (173 Water St., 902/368-4444; July–Aug. daily 8 A.M.–9 P.M., spring and fall daily 9 A.M.–6 P.M., winter Mon.–Fri. 9 A.M.–6 P.M.) your first stop.

GETTING ORIENTED

The city, small as it is, may be baffling for a new visitor because of the way historic and newer streets converge. The town began with a handful of harborfront blocks. The centuries have contributed a confusing jumble of other roads that feed into the historic area from all sorts of angles.

From either direction, the **TransCanada Highway** (Route 1) will take you right into the heart of town. From the west, it crosses the North River, turns south at the University of Prince Edward Island campus and becomes University Avenue. From the east, take the Water Street exit to reach the information center.

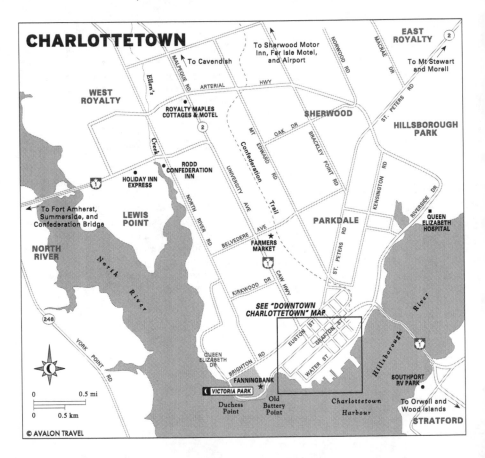

Extending from the harbor to Euston Street, the commercial area is pleasantly compact, attractive, and easily covered on foot. **Old Charlottetown** (or Old Charlotte Town, depending on who's describing the area) has been restored with rejuvenated buildings and brick walkways, lighted at night with gas lamps.

The most-sought-after residential areas, with large stately houses, rim Victoria Park and North River Road. Working-class neighborhoods fan out farther north beyond Grafton Street and are marked with small pastel-painted houses set close to the streets.

DOWNTOWN
◖ Founders' Hall

Years of restoration saw a historic railway building transformed into Founders' Hall (6 Prince St., 902/368-1864; adult $7, senior $6, child $4), Charlottetown's number-one attraction. Located on the harbor beside the information center, this state-of-the-art facility combines the latest technology, dynamic audiovisuals, holo-visuals, and interactive displays to create a very different museum experience. You'll enter the Time Tunnel and travel back to 1864, when the Fathers of Confederation first met to discuss the union of Canada. You'll proceed through history, from the formation of each province and territory to modern times. Founders' Hall hours vary (Feb.–mid-May daily 10 A.M.–3 P.M., mid-May–mid-June daily 10 A.M.–5 P.M., mid-June–end of June daily 9 A.M.–6 P.M., July–mid-Aug. daily 8:30 A.M.–8 P.M., mid-Aug.–early Oct. daily 8:30 A.M.–6 P.M., early Oct.–Nov. daily 9 A.M.–3 P.M.).

Downtown Waterfront

A rejuvenation project has seen much improvement in the downtown waterfront precinct, much of it spurred on by the establishment of Founders' Hall. The adjacent **Confederation Landing Park** is rimmed by a seaside boardwalk and filled with pleasant gardens and well-trimmed grass. The park is integrated with **Peake's Wharf**, where the Fathers of Confederation arrived on the island. This is

© ANDREW HEMPSTEAD

Founders' Hall

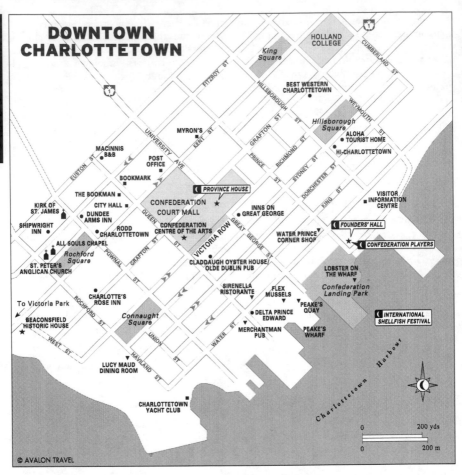

now a tourist hub of sorts with restaurants and shops, and tour boats wait to take interested visitors on sightseeing trips.

(Province House

The nation of Canada began at Province House (corner Grafton St. and Great George St., 902/566-7626; June–Sept. daily 9 A.M.–5 P.M., Oct.–May Mon.–Fri. 9 A.M.–5 P.M.; free), four blocks up Great George Street from the harbor. Now protected as a national historic site, the buff sandstone neoclassical edifice at the high point of downtown was erected in 1847

to house the island's colonial legislature. It quickly became the center of public life on the island. It was the site of lavish balls and state functions, including the historic 1864 conference on federal union. The provincial legislature still convenes here; meetings are in session between mid-February and early May for 5 to 17 weeks, depending on how much provincial government haggling is underway.

In the late 1970s, Parks Canada undertook restoration of the age-begrimed building, a five-year task completed in 1983. Layers of paint came off the front columns. The double-hung windows throughout were refitted with glass panes from an old greenhouse in New Brunswick. About 10 percent of the original furnishings remained in the building before restoration and were retained. Most of the rest were replaced by period antiques obtained in the other provinces and the northeastern United States. A flowered rug was woven for Confederation Chamber, where the Fathers of Confederation convened. Every nook and corner was refurbished and polished until the interior gleamed. Today, Province House is one of Atlantic Canada's most significant public buildings.

Confederation Centre of the Arts

Confederation Centre of the Arts (145 Richmond St., 902/628-1864) is the other half of the imposing complex shared by Province House. The promenades, edged with places to sit, are great places for people watching, and kids like to skateboard on the walkways.

The center opened in 1964 to mark the centennial of the Charlottetown Conference, as the confederation meeting became known in Canadian history. It's a great hulk of a place, compatible with its historic neighbor in its design and coloring. The center houses an art gallery, the provincial library, four theaters, and a café. The emphasis at the **Confederation Centre Art Gallery** (mid-June–Sept. daily 9 A.M.–5 P.M., Oct.–mid-June Wed.–Sat. 11 A.M.–5 P.M. and Sun. 1–5 P.M.; free) is the work of Canadian artists—expect to see some of island artist Robert Harris's paintings and Lucy Maud Montgomery's original manuscripts. A gift shop stocks wares by the cream of PEI's artisans.

All Souls' Chapel

A few blocks west of Queen Street, this remarkable chapel next to **St. Peter's Anglican Church** (Rochford St., 902/628-1376; daily 8 A.M.–6 P.M.; free) was a joint Harris family creation. The architect William Harris styled it in island sandstone with a dark walnut interior. His brother Robert painted the murals

and deftly mixed family members and friends among the religious figures.

Beaconsfield Historic House

This bright yellow 25-room mansion (2 Kent St., 902/368-6603; tours July–Aug. daily 10 A.M.–5 P.M.; adult $4.50, child $3.50) was built in 1877 from a William Critchlow Harris design. The building has survived more than a century of varied use as a family home, a shelter for "friendless women," a YWCA, and a nurses' residence. It was rescued in 1973 by the PEI Museum and Heritage Foundation, which turned it into foundation headquarters and a heritage museum. A good bookstore is on the first level, and genealogical archives are kept across the hall and also upstairs. Outside, you can sit on the wide front porch overlooking the harbor across the long lawn—it's a great place to have tea and scones.

◖ Victoria Park

Victoria Park, adjacent to Beaconsfield House, reigns as one of Charlottetown's prettiest settings, with 16 wooded and grassy hectares overlooking the bay at Battery Point. The greenery spreads out across the peninsula tip; to get there follow Kent Street as it turns into Park Roadway. The park's rolling terrain is the result of moraines, heaps of gravelly deposits left behind by ice-age glaciers.

Joggers like the park's winding paths, and birders find abundant yellow warblers, purple finches, and downy woodpeckers nesting in the maples, firs, oaks, pines, and birches. The white palatial mansion overlooking the water is Fanningbank (Government House), the lieutenant governor's private residence—nice to look at, but it's closed to the public.

BEYOND DOWNTOWN
Farmers' Market

The Farmers' Market (100 Belvedere Ave., 902/626-3373; July–Aug. Sat. 9 A.M.–2 P.M. and Wed. 10 A.M.–5 P.M.) is across from the university campus. The indoor market holds about 40 vendors selling everything from flowers and crafts to baked goods, produce, and fish.

Fort Amherst-Port-la-Joye National Historic Site

Just four kilometers across the harbor from downtown, but a 35-minute drive via Routes 1 and 19, Fort Amherst–Port-la-Joye National Historic Site protects the site of the island's first European settlement. It all began in 1720, when three French ships sailed into Port-la-Joye (today's Charlottetown Harbour) carrying some 300 settlers. Most of them moved to the north shore and established fishing villages, but the rest remained here at the military outpost.

Within just four years, adverse conditions had driven out most of the French. The British burned Port-la-Joye in 1745 and took control of the island. The French later returned to rebuild their capital but were compelled to surrender Port-la-Joye to a superior British force in 1758. The British renamed the post Fort Amherst. After the British established the new capital at Charlottetown, Fort Amherst fell quickly into disrepair, and now no buildings remain. The grounds, which have picnic tables, are open June–August.

OUTDOOR ACTIVITIES

Those looking for easy walking gravitate to the waterfront at the southwestern end of downtown. This is the starting point for a paved trail that extends to Old Battery Point and Victoria Park. While this area is also popular for biking, cyclists looking for longer rides will be impressed at how easy it is to reach the rural landscape beyond city limits. From downtown, the ride out to Brackley Beach (45 kilometers) is a good destination for a full-day ride.

MacQueen's Bike Shop (430 Queen St., 902/368-2453) provides complete bike and accessory rental and repairs and can also arrange cycle-touring packages. **Smooth Cycle** (330 University Ave., 902/566-5530) also offers rentals and repairs as well as drop-offs for the Confederation Trail. Both companies charge from $25 per day for a road bike.

Entertainment and Events

Charlottetown once rolled up the sidewalks at night, but in recent years a rousing nightlife and pub scene has emerged, centered on drinking and dancing. Last call for drinks is at 1:30 A.M.; the doors lock at 2 A.M. For complete listings of all that's happening around the city, pick up the free weekly *Buzz* or the weekend editions of *The Guardian* newspaper.

PUBS AND BARS

Peake's Quay (1 Great George St., 902/368-1330; daily from 11 A.M.) has a prime waterfront location, making it popular with both locals and visitors. While the service is often blasé, it's a good family-friendly environment with inexpensive food and lots of outdoor seating. Look for live music most weekends after 9 P.M. **Olde Dublin Pub** (131 Sydney St., 902/892-6992) has a popular deck and offers Celtic and Irish music Thursday–Saturday for a $5 cover charge.

Mavor's (145 Richmond St., 902/628-6107; Mon.–Sat. 11 A.M.–10 P.M.), in the Confederation Centre of the Arts, is a colorful space with over 40 wines by the glass, top-notch martinis, and a thoughtful menu of light meals under $15.

The **Selkirk Lounge** (Delta Prince Edward, 18 Queen St., 902/894-1208; daily noon–11 P.M.) is a sophisticated space within one of the city's top hotels. Piano players perform Tuesday–Saturday evenings; martinis and specialty coffees are highlights on a long menu of drinks.

The **42nd St. Lounge** (125 Sydney St., 902/566-4620) is another good choice for a quiet drink and conversation; ask one of the affable bartenders for a cognac, kick back in one of the overstuffed chairs, and listen to soft jazz on the sound system. Highly recommended.

NIGHTCLUBS

A mainstay of the club scene is **Velvet Underground** (166 Prince St., 902/628-6898). Music plays Tuesday–Saturday, with the Saturday dance party attracting the biggest crowd. As closet-like as Myron's is cavernous, **Baba's Lounge** (upstairs at 81 University Ave., 902/892-7377) is a "hipoisie" hangout extraordinaire. "Intimate" is an understatement here; bodies writhe to the rhythm on a dance floor about the size of a postage stamp. Expect live music ranging from slightly alternative to modern rock.

PERFORMING ARTS

The **Confederation Centre of the Arts** (145 Richmond St., 902/566-1267) is the performing-arts capital of the province and the site of the **Charlottetown Festival,** which runs from mid-June to late September. The festival is best known for the *Anne of Green Gables* musical; tickets cost $50–70. Also on the bill are repertory productions in the center's main theater and cabaret-style productions at the **MacKenzie Theatre,** the festival's second stage at University Avenue and Grafton Street.

FESTIVALS AND EVENTS

June

The June to mid-October **Charlottetown Festival** (902/628-1864, www.confederationcentre.com) presents musical theater and cabaret at the Confederation Centre and the nearby MacKenzie Theatre. Two musicals are presented, including one centering on *Anne of Green Gables.*

July

The **Canada Day** long weekend (first weekend in July) is celebrated on the waterfront with a food fair, nationalistic displays, buskers, island music, and the **Festival of Lights** fireworks display.

Organized by the Charlottetown Yacht Club, **Race Week** (902/892-9065, www.cyc .pe.ca) runs Wednesday–Saturday in the middle of July. The program revolves around yacht races for various classes of boats, with other scheduled activities including shore games and nightly entertainment. Even if you're not involved in the event, watching the yachts racing across the harbor is a sight to behold.

August

The mid-August **Old Home Week** (902/629-6623, www.oldhomeweekpei.com), Atlantic Canada's largest agricultural exposition, centers on Charlottetown Driving Park, northeast of downtown along Kensington Road. The city unofficially shuts down for the week-ending **Gold Cup Parade** through the streets of Charlottetown—said to be Atlantic Canada's biggest and best-attended parade. Daily grounds admission is a reasonable adult $7, child $4.

September
◖ INTERNATIONAL SHELLFISH FESTIVAL

Summer ends with the International Shellfish Festival (www.peishellfish.com), over the third weekend of September. Festivities along the waterfront include an oyster-shucking contest, a Chowder Challenge, "touch tanks," cooking classes, the World is Your Oyster children's program, sock-hanging, and chefs from the local culinary institute sharing their cooking skills with the public.

Shopping

Centrally located and the largest city by far, Charlottetown is the island's shopping hub. Downtown is a pleasant blend of old and new shopping experiences, although the main concentration of shopping malls is north of downtown along University Avenue. Stores catering to islanders are normally open Monday–Saturday from about 9 A.M. to 5 P.M. while touristy ones open later in July and August and also operate on Sunday.

ARTS AND CRAFTS

Local artists capture the island in masterful watercolors, acrylics, oils, and sculpture. Local crafts include finely made quilts, knits and woolens, stained glass, jewelry, pewter, pottery, and handsome furniture. The Anne doll is the most popular souvenir, and it's produced in innumerable variations for as little as $20 to as much as $800.

An exquisite handmade quilt costs $400–800—seldom a bargain. But well-crafted quilts are sturdily constructed and will last a lifetime with good care. Sweaters ($75–300) are especially high quality. One of the best sources is **Northern Watters Knitwear,** which operates a downtown factory outlet (150 Richmond St., 902/566-5850).

The **P.E.I. Crafts Council** is a driving force behind local arts and crafts. It counts about 100 provincial craftspeople among its esteemed ranks. **Island Crafts Shop** (156 Richmond St., 902/892-5152) functions as the council members' outlet. A thorough browse among quilts, glassware, sculpture, clothing, knitted apparel, and jewelry ad infinitum will provide you an insight into what's available in the city and province. Craftspeople demonstrate their trades at the shop from time to time. The wares here tend to be one-of-a-kind. If you don't see exactly what you want, you could go directly to the maker; the membership list is available at the shop.

Accommodations and Camping

You'll find every kind of lodging, from plain budget places to sumptuous expensive rooms, in Charlottetown's 100-plus lodgings. Also, unlike elsewhere in the province, most are open year-round.

Unless noted otherwise, prices given below are for a double room; sales tax is not included in these prices.

DOWNTOWN
Under $50

Charlottetown's lone hostel is **HI-Charlottetown** (60 Hillsborough St., 902/367-5749, www.hihostels.ca; dorm beds $27–30, $65–70 d), a converted residential home just two blocks east of Province House. Facilities include a living room with a fireplace, a recreation room, and wireless Internet.

$50-100

Operated by the same owners as HI-Charlottetown and in the same vicinity, **Aloha Tourist Home** (234 Sydney St., 902/892-9944 or 866/892-9944, www.alohaamigo.com; $56–68 s or d) is an inexpensive downtown accommodation for those looking for private rooms. The renovated home has four guest rooms with single or double beds, two shared bathrooms, a shared kitchen, a lounge area, and free wireless Internet throughout.

One of the least expensive of Charlottetown's historic accommodations with en suite rooms is **MacInnis Bed and Breakfast** (80 Euston St., 902/892-6725), a homey, centrally located choice with a veranda that overlooks pleasant gardens. It offers two regular guest rooms ($85 s or d) and a top-floor one-bedroom suite ($135 s or d).

$100-150

The elegant 1860s 🍁 **Shipwright Inn** (51 Fitzroy St., 902/368-1905 or 888/306-9966, www.shipwrightinn.com; $149–249 s or d) was originally the home of shipbuilder James Douse. The inn has eight rooms and suites, all with private baths and furnished in richly colored nautical themes (my favorite is the Chart Room, with an 1830s four-poster walnut bed, heavy drapes, and historic sea charts on the walls). Rates include a full breakfast.

What makes **Elmwood Heritage Inn** (121 North River Rd., 902/368-3310 or 877/933-3310, www.elmwoodinn.pe.ca; $149–259 including breakfast) stand out is the setting. Still within easy walking distance of downtown, it is in a parklike setting, surrounded by mature gardens and with a row of stately elm trees leading up from the wrought-iron entry gates to the front door. Built for the grandson of Samuel Cunard in 1889, the mansion boasts 28 very Victorian guest rooms, many with jetted tubs and fireplaces.

Best Western Charlottetown (238 Grafton St., 902/892-2461 or 800/528-1234, www.bestwesternatlantic.com; $145–185 s or d) is a three-block jaunt from Province House. It has 143 midsized rooms fronting both sides of the street, connected beneath the road by a tunnel. Facilities include a pub-style restaurant, indoor pool, sauna, hot tub, and launderette.

$150-200

A restored Queen Anne Revival mansion awash with antiques, **Dundee Arms Inn** (200 Pownal St., 902/892-2496 or 877/638-6333, www.dundeearms.com; $145–220 s, $155–230 d) has been taking in guests since the early 1970s. Conveniently located between downtown and Victoria Park, its other pluses include a good restaurant and comfortable beds. Note that half the 18 rooms are in a modern addition out back of the original home, but these are still stylishly decorated and come with wireless Internet, bathrobes, and more.

Charlotte's Rose Inn (11 Grafton St., www.charlottesrose.ca, 902/892-3699 or 888/237-3699) is a three-story 1884 home on a quiet residential street. Original hardwood floors, high ceilings, and Victorian-era furnishings add to the charm. The four en suite guest rooms rent for $155–205 s or d, including a cooked breakfast.

Over $200

A few steps from Province House, 🍁 **Inns on Great George** (58 Great George St., 902/892-0606 or 800/361-1118, www.innsongreatgeorge.com; $209–349 s or d) comprises 53 guest rooms spread through 13 beautifully restored buildings dating to as early as 1811. The lobby is in a building that was originally known as the Pavilion Hotel, at the corner of Great George and Sydney Streets. It was here that the Fathers of Confederation stayed during the 1864 Charlottetown Conference. This building also has a large lounge area and a fine-dining restaurant. Rooms in this and buildings running up Great George Street and beyond have been beautifully restored, with the addition of modern amenities like air-conditioning and high-speed Internet access.

Rodd Charlottetown (75 Kent St., 902/894-7371 or 800/565-7633, www.roddhotelsandresorts.com; $230 s or d) is a grand red-brick 1931 Georgian gem with magnificent woodwork and furnishings made by island craftspeople. It offers 115 rooms and suites and a restaurant, whirlpool, indoor pool, and rooftop patio. As always with these top-end properties, check the website for the best deals.

Like the nearby Confederation Centre, the **Delta Prince Edward** (18 Queen St., 902/566-2222 or 888/890-3222, www.deltahotels.com; $240 s or d) stands out for its boxy look amid the gracious buildings of downtown. Inside are 211 well-decorated rooms. The more expensive Delta Rooms have king beds and water views. It offers all the amenities of a full-service hotel, including underground valet parking ($19 per day), a day spa, a fitness room, an indoor pool, a lounge, and a restaurant. Disregard the rack rates and check online—you should find packages that include accommodations and either theater tickets or greens fees for around $200 d.

© ANDREW HEMPSTEAD

Rodd Charlottetown, a grand 1931 Georgian hotel

NORTH OF DOWNTOWN

Staying downtown has its perks, but if you're looking for a well-priced motel room or are traveling with a family, staying on the north side is a good alternative.

$50-100

Sherwood Motor Inn (281 Brackley Point Rd., 902/892-1622 or 800/567-1622) is a reliable cheapie opposite the airport turnoff eight kilometers north of downtown. It comprises a strip of dated motel rooms ($65–75 s or d) and a newer two-story building filled with air-conditioned rooms ($85–105 s or d).

A little closer toward the city, **Fair Isle Motel** (Rte. 2, 902/368-8259 or 800/309-8259; Apr.–Nov.; $40–56 s, $50–66 d), an old roadside motel where rooms overlook landscaped gardens. If you've picked up fresh seafood at Lobster on the Wharf, take advantage of this motel's barbecues for a great outdoor dinner.

I doubt too many Canadian capitals boast a cottage complex surrounded by expansive lawns within city limits, but Charlottetown does, in the form of (**Royalty Maples Cottages & Motel** (Rte. 2, 902/368-1030, www.royaltymaples.com; May–Nov.), which is one kilometer north of the junction of Routes 1 and 2. The 10 one- and two-bedroom cottages ($95–125 s or d) each have a full kitchen, living area, and air-conditioning. Six motel rooms go for $75 s or d per night.

$100-150

At the busy intersection of Routes 1 and 2, four kilometers north of downtown along University Avenue, is **Rodd Confederation Inn** (TransCanada Hwy., 902/892-2481 or 800/565-7633, www.roddhotelsandresorts.com; $125–160 s or d). This spread-out property features 31 regular guest rooms and 31 suites (the latter are better value). Other facilities include a heated outdoor pool, playground, pub, and restaurant.

$150-200

The **Holiday Inn Express** (200 TransCanada Hwy., 902/892-1201 or 800/465-4329, www.ichotelsgroup.com; $155–210 s or d) maintains the same standards and facilities expected of this worldwide chain. The modern rooms have air-conditioning and high-speed Internet access, and rates include a continental breakfast. Families can take advantage of children's suites, complete with Nintendo systems and bunk beds separate from the main bedroom. Other amenities include an indoor pool and a sundeck.

CAMPGROUNDS
East

The only campground within city limits is **Southport RV Park** (20 Stratford Rd., Stratford, 902/569-2287; mid-May–mid-Oct.; $22–34 per night). This facility sprawls along the east bank of the Hillsborough River, a short five-minute drive east from downtown. It has tent and full-hookup spaces, a Laundromat, a kitchen shelter, and views back across the water to downtown.

West

[**Holiday Haven Campground** (Rte. 248, 2 km east of Cornwall, 902/566-2421, www .holidayhaven.pe.ca; June–early Oct.) spreads across 25 beautiful hectares along the West River. Amenities include an outdoor swimming pool, a playground, hayrides, showers, a launderette, and a kitchen shelter. All sites are $28 per night.

Follow the TransCanada Highway west from downtown toward the Confederation Bridge and you'll pass the entrance to **Strathgartney Provincial Park** (Rte. 1, Churchill, 902/675-7476; mid-June–early Sept.) after 20 kilometers. The park's 55 hectares encompass inland woodlands spliced by (and providing delightful views of) the Strathgartney River (with fishing). Facilities include unserviced campsites ($22) and two-way hookup sites ($25), hiking trails, hot showers, a launderette, kitchen shelters, and a nearby campers store.

Food

Island fare is *good,* and while it centers on homegrown produce and seafood from the surrounding ocean, everything comes together in the capital, with an excellent array of dining opportunities for all budgets. The center of the eating action is **Victoria Row,** a block of vintage buildings along Richmond Street between Queen and Great George Streets. The street is pedestrian-only through summer. The restaurants set up outdoor tables while musicians play to the assembled crowd of diners.

Even if you're not in town for the **International Shellfish Festival** (third weekend of September), you'll find local delicacies such as lobster and Malpeque oysters on menus throughout the city. Local produce and dairy products are delicious. Chefs make the most of island-grown succulent berries, locally produced maple syrup, and thick, sweet honey.

CAFÉS

On pedestrian-only Victoria Row, **Cafe Diem** (128 Richmond St., 902/892-0494; Apr.–Oct. daily 8 A.M.–10 P.M.) is centrally located for a break from sightseeing. On the menu are dozens of coffee concoctions, light lunches such as sandwiches and bagels, and a tempting array of sweet treats. This is also the city's most central Internet café.

Just Juicin' (62 Queen St., 902/894-3104; Mon.–Sat. 8 A.M.–5 P.M., Sun. noon–5 P.M.) started out mixing up fresh juices but now also offers the healthy (smoked salmon bagels) to the heavy (rich chocolate cake).

At the Confederation Centre of the Arts, **[** **Mavor's** (145 Richmond St., 902/628-6107; daily 8 A.M.–8 P.M.) is a striking room where you can get your fill of Starbucks coffee, complete with the fancy names. The kitchen opens daily except Sunday at 11 A.M., serving up fresh and wholesome food, with ethnic influences showing through in dishes such as blue mussels steamed in Thai curry broth. Also good: the thin-crust smoked salmon pizza ($12) and sweet potato wedges with a side of sour cream ($6.50).

Beanz Espresso Bar (38 University Ave., 902/892-8797; Mon.–Fri. 6:30 A.M.–6 P.M., Sat. 8 A.M.–6 P.M., Sun. 9 A.M.–4 P.M.) gets rave reviews for its coffee, but the soups, salads, sandwiches, and old-fashioned pastries draw me back every time I'm in Charlottetown.

SEAFOOD

[**Flex Mussels** (2 Lower Water St., 902/569-0200; daily noon–midnight) is a unique and tasty stop. Mussels are the specialty. They are steamed open to order in one of 50 flavors, including Parisienne (Pernod, tarragon, and basil), Wild Turkey (roasted corn, green onions, kumquats, and bourbon), Maine (baby clams, cream, and parsley), and Cajun (spicy Creole sauce, red wine, shrimp, and okra). The cost is $12–16 per pound, with delicious fries a worthwhile $4.50 extra. Want to watch a mussel grow? Then check out the company's mussel-cam at www.flexmussels.com.

Water Prince Corner Shop (141 Water St., 902/368-3212; May–Oct. daily 9 A.M.–8 P.M., July–Aug. until 10 P.M.) looks like a regular convenience store from the outside, but inside the ocean-blue clapboard building is a casual dining space where the emphasis is on fresh seafood at reasonable prices. It's all good—lobster burgers, lobster dinners, seafood chowder, steamed clams, and more.

Fishbones (136 Richmond St., 902/628-6569; daily from 11 A.M. for lunch and dinner) is a fresh, casual restaurant along pedestrian-only Victoria Row. Start at the oyster bar before moving on to a set menu of contemporary creations such as the grilled salmon brushed with maple butter. Other highlights include a rich seafood stew and baked halibut topped with salsa. Mains are in the $18–27 range.

The **Claddagh Oyster House** (131 Sydney St., 902/892-9661; Mon.–Fri. for lunch, daily for dinner) is authentically Irish, starting with owner Liam Dolan from County Galway. Seafood is the specialty ($17–30), with the Lobster spaghetti ($29) a rich-tasting splurge.

For its harborfront location alone, **Lobster on the Wharf** (2 Prince St., 902/368-2888; May–Oct. 11:30 A.M.–10 P.M.) is a longtime favorite with visitors and locals alike from its waterfront foundations, but the venerable restaurant has been rebuilt, complete with an extra level and a large deck. As the name suggests, lobster is the specialty (the lobster risotto is delicious), but the fish-and-chips in tempura batter ($18) is also excellent.

PUB DINING

Taking full advantage of its harborfront locale is the upstairs **Peake's Quay** (1 Great George St., 902/368-1330; daily from 11 A.M.), with informal indoor and outdoor dining and an enviable seafood selection ($11–22); try the scallops sauced with honey butter. Peake's Quay is also arguably the hottest nightspot in town, drawing locals, landlubber tourists, and yachties (who tie up at the adjacent marina) alike to see and be seen while listening or dancing to top touring bands, so plan on dining early.

The Merchantman Pub (23 Queen St., 902/892-9150; Mon.–Sat. from 11:30 A.M.) has a nice atmosphere, a wide-ranging menu that includes some Thai and Cajun dishes, and a good beer selection. But the place seems a little overpriced, probably due to its location across the street from the upscale Delta Prince Edward.

CANADIAN

The **Lucy Maud Dining Room** (4 Sydney St., 902/894-6868; Tues.–Fri. 11:30 A.M.–1:30 P.M., Tues.–Sat. 6–8 P.M.) is part of the Culinary Institute of Canada, a respected school that attracts students from across the country. Turn a blind eye to the rather institutional room, concentrate on the water views, and sit back to enjoy enthusiastic service and well-priced meals that blend contemporary and Continental. Expect to pay $35 for a four-course meal.

If you want to dine in one of the city's best restaurants but don't want to pay for an expensive dinner, eat breakfast at **The Selkirk** (Delta Prince Edward, 18 Queen St., 902/894-1208; Mon.–Sat. 7 A.M.–2:30 P.M. and 6–9 P.M., Sun. 11 A.M.–2 P.M.). The buffet is $17, or try dishes as traditional as fish cakes with baked beans ($14) or as creative as lobster eggs Benedict ($18). Things go upscale in the evening. That's when you can order pork tenderloin ravioli or smoked duck and asparagus salad to start, followed by pan-fried arctic char topped with fruit salsa or salmon marinated in whiskey and maple syrup and then grilled on a cedar plank. Starters are mostly under $15 and mains range $25–33.

The **Griffon Room** (Dundee Arms Inn, 200 Pownal St., 902/892-2496; daily for breakfast, lunch, and dinner) is away from the tourist crush within a restored three-story manor that combines an old-fashioned setting with elegantly conceived fine cuisine emphasizing red meats and seafood. If you feel like a break from seafood, you won't regret it with the roast pork tenderloin topped with peach relish. Mains are $21–32.

ITALIAN

Sirenella Ristorante (83 Water St., 902/628-2271; Mon.–Fri. 11:30 A.M.–2 P.M., Mon.–Sat. 5 A.M.–10 P.M.) serves up traditional Northern Italian food in a simple but classy setting. The scallop, shrimp, and hot sauce linguine is delicious. The wine list is dominated by Italian reds and whites. Mains range $13–27. A children's menu and patio add to the appeal.

ICE CREAM

Ice-cream fanciers whoop it up at **Ⓒ Cow's,** a local ice-cream company that is renowned as much for its creamy treats wrapped in handmade waffle cones as for its colorful merchandise. Downtown outlets include opposite the Confederation Centre (corner of Queen St. and Grafton St., 902/892-6969) and at Peakes Wharf (902/566-4886). On your way off the island, you can also indulge at Gateway Village or aboard the ferry.

Information and Services

TOURIST INFORMATION

Charlottetown's main **Visitor Information Centre** is right beside the harbor (173 Water St., 902/368-4444; July–Aug. daily 8 A.M.–9 P.M., spring and fall daily 9 A.M.–6 P.M., winter Mon.–Fri. 9 A.M.–6 P.M.) answers questions and stocks a good supply of literature about the province and Charlottetown. Inside city hall, at the corner of Kent and Queen Streets, is a smaller seasonal information booth. The official island tourism website (www.peiplay.com) is a good source for advance planning.

LIBRARY

Access to the centrally located **Confederation Centre Public Library** (902/368-4642; Mon. and Fri.–Sat. 10 A.M.–5 P.M., Tues.–Thurs. 10 A.M.–9 P.M., Sun. 1–5 P.M.) is from Richmond Street. It has a solid collection of island literature, newspapers from across North America, and free public Internet access.

BOOKSTORES

Bookmark (172 Queen St., 902/566-4888; Mon.–Fri. 8:30 A.M.–9 P.M., Sat. 9 A.M.–5:30 P.M., Sun. noon–5 P.M.) is an excellent locally owned bookstore in the heart of downtown. You can pick up coffee-table books, *Anne of Green Gables,* and field guides.

For island literature and especially architecture and history coverage, check out the bookshop at **Beaconsfield Historic House** (2 Kent St., 902/368-6600; July–Aug. daily 10 A.M.–5 P.M., Sept.–June Wed.–Thurs. noon–5 P.M.).

The Bookman (177 Queen St., 902/892-8872) carries new, used, and rare books.

HEALTH AND SAFETY

Queen Elizabeth Hospital is on Riverside Drive (902/894-2200). For **police** call 902/566-7112.

POST AND INTERNET

The main **post office** is at 135 Kent Street (902/628-4400).

Most accommodations in the capital offer wireless or high-speed Internet access, or head to the **Confederation Centre Public Library** (902/368-4642; Mon. and Fri.–Sat. 10 A.M.–5 P.M., Tues.–Thurs. 10 A.M.–9 P.M., Sun. 1–5 P.M.). Across from the library, **Cafe Diem** (128 Richmond St., 902/892-0494; daily 8 A.M.–10 P.M.) has a row of computers along an upstairs indoor balcony; Internet access costs $6 per half hour.

OTHER SERVICES

Coin laundries are plentiful; they're generally open daily 8 A.M.–11 P.M. Among them, **Better Than Home Laundromat** (73 St. Peters Rd., 902/628-1994) and **Mid Town Laundromat** (238 University Ave., 902/628-2329) offer drop-off service.

For all your digital camera needs, head to **PEI Photo Lab** (55 Queen St., 902/892-5107).

Getting There and Around

GETTING THERE

Charlottetown Airport is eight kilometers north of downtown along Brackley Point Road. **Air Canada** (888/247-2262) has direct flights from Toronto, Montréal, Ottawa, and Halifax while **WestJet** (888/937-8538) flies in from Toronto.

Though open daily 24 hours, it's a small airport sans banks or a duty-free shop. For sightseeing and other information, use the free phone line to the tourist office. Taxis wait outside during flight arrivals and charge about $12 for one person or $15 for two for the 15-minute drive to town. Avis, Budget, Hertz, and National rent vehicles at the airport, but their counters are not staffed between flights.

GETTING AROUND

Use **Charlottetown Transit** (902/566-9962) to get anywhere in Greater Charlottetown for $2; buses run weekdays only.

Charlottetown taxis are plentiful; you'll pay $4–6 to get almost anywhere downtown. Taxis cruise the streets or wait at major downtown hotels. Taxi companies include **City Cab** (902/892-6567), **Co-op** (902/892-1111), and **Yellow Cab** (902/566-6666).

Local rental-car agencies include **Avis** (902/892-3706), **Budget** (902/566-5525), **Hertz** (902/966-5566), and **National** (902/628-6990).

TOURS

◖ Confederation Players

The Confederation Players are keen local historians who dress in period costume to conduct walking tours of downtown Charlottetown from Founders' Hall (6 Prince St., 902/368-1864) mid-June through August. The regular one-hour tour departs daily at 11 A.M., 1 P.M., and 3:30 P.M.; the one-hour tour for French speakers departs at 1 P.M. The Ghostly Realm Tour departs Tuesday–Saturday at 7:30 P.M. All tours cost a reasonable $10 per person.

Bus and Boat Tours

Abegweit Tours (902/894-9966) operates the red double-decker bus that lopes through Charlottetown on sightseeing tours ($10 for a one-hour tour). The bus stops at Confederation Centre on Queen and Grafton Streets, and it runs mid-June through September daily 10:30 A.M.–6:15 P.M.

Peake's Wharf Boat Tours (902/629-1864) operates a covered 42-foot boat from Peake's Wharf, at the foot of Great George Street. Options include a 70-minute sightseeing cruise (1 P.M.; $22), a 2.5-hour seal-watching cruise (2:30 P.M.; $30), and 70-minute evening and sunset cruises (6:30 P.M. and 8 P.M.; both $25). The tours run June to early September.

The South Shore

From Charlottetown, Route 1 (TransCanada Highway) whisks travelers 56 kilometers southwest to Borden–Carleton, from where the Confederation Bridge provides a link to the rest of Canada. If you're arriving on the island via the bridge, consider veering off Route 1 at DeSable and following scenic Route 19 along the South Shore to Rocky Point and Fort Amherst–Port-la-Joye National Historic Site for views of the city skyline across sparkling Charlottetown Harbour.

VICTORIA

Victoria (pop. 200), 40 kilometers west of Charlottetown, marks Queens County's southwestern corner. The town owed its start to shipbuilding, and by 1870 Victoria ranked as one of the island's busiest ports. As the demand for wooden ships faded, the seaport turned to cattle shipping—herds of cattle were driven down the coastal slopes to water's edge, where they were hoisted with slings onto waiting ships.

Today Victoria shows just a shadow of its former luster. The seaport slipped off the commercial circuit decades ago, and the settlement shrank to a handful of waterfront blocks. Happily, island craftspeople discovered the serene setting. It's still a quiet place where the fishing fleet puts out to sea early in the morning as the mist rises off the strait. But now the peaceful seaport also holds a modest arts colony, with outlets along the main street.

Victoria Playhouse

If an evening at the theater sounds good, make plans to attend the **Victoria Playhouse** (Howard St., 902/658-2025, www.victoriaplayhouse.com), a repertory theater that showcases historically themed comedy and drama (adult $24, senior $22, child $18), as well as concerts of jazz and folk music.

Accommodations

Next to the Victoria Playhouse, **Victoria Village Inn** (Howard St., 902/658-2483 or 866/658-2483, www.victoriavillageinn.com; $90–145 s or d) is an 1870s inn that was originally built for a sea captain. Awash with lustrous antiques, it offers four comfortable guest units—one with three bedrooms. The inn also has a restaurant open daily in summer for dinner.

Kitty-corner to the theater, the **Orient Hotel** (Main St., 902/658-2503 or 800/565-6743; mid-May–mid-Oct.; $80–150 s or d) has been taking in guests since 1900. It features a few smallish guest rooms (from $80) and larger suites ($130–150). Rates include a delicious breakfast, and tea and coffee throughout the day.

Food

Enterprising locals remodeled the old general store and post office and opened ◖ **Landmark Café** (12 Main St., 902/658-2286; June–Sept. daily 11:30 A.M.–9 P.M.). You can't go wrong with any of the fresh seasonal cooking, but the soups and meat pies are especially good.

Walk out on Victoria Wharf to reach **Ruthie's Lobster House** (902/658-2200; June–Sept. daily 11:30 A.M.–2:30 P.M. and 5–9 P.M.), a haven for seafood and steaks. The adjacent **Ruthie's Pub** has live music most weekends.

Two kilometers east of the main wharf is **Morning Star Fisheries** (902/658-3045; summer daily 10 A.M.–7 P.M.), where you can purchase a cooked lobster and then enjoy it at the picnic area in nearby **Victoria Provincial Park.**

BORDEN-CARLETON

The twin villages of Borden–Carleton, 56 kilometers west of Charlottetown, are the closest point to mainland Canada, and so have always been an important transportation hub. Back in the late 1700s, iceboats carrying mail and passengers crossed Northumberland Strait when the island was icebound from December to early spring. The voyages were filled with hair-raising tales of survival, and the iceboats—rigged with fragile sails and runners—were often trapped in the strait's ice. It wasn't until 1916 that the first vehicle ferry made the crossing, but in 1997, the Confederation Bridge opened and the ferry service was discontinued.

Since the opening of the bridge, Borden–Carleton, 56 kilometers west of Charlottetown, has seen much development as thousands of travelers peeling off the bridge come looking for food and information, and those leaving stop to stock up with last-minute souvenirs.

Gateway Village

As you descend the final span of Confederation Bridge, 12-hectare Gateway Village soon comes into view. It is designed especially for bridge travelers, but well worth visiting even if you're on your way back to the mainland. With the theme of an island streetscape of the early 1900s, the shops are filled with island souvenirs, some tacky (T-shirts, Christmas decorations, etc.), some tasty (fresh lobster), and some trendy (wine from Rossignol Estate Winery). The epicenter for new arrivals is the cavernous **Gateway Village Visitor Information Centre** (902/437-8570; daily 9 A.M.–6 P.M., spring and fall until 8 P.M., summer until 10 P.M.), where friendly staff will help sort out the best way to spend your time while on the island. Displays within the center focus on various island experiences. Outside, amid the café tables and wandering visitors, free musical performances and craft demonstrations add to the appeal.

Confederation Bridge

If you arrived in Borden–Carlton via the Confederation Bridge, you enjoyed a free ride. If you're leaving the island, it's time to pay. The toll is $41.50 per vehicle including passengers. Payment is collected at toll booths on the island side of the bridge. Have cash, credit card, or debit card ready.

Accommodations

Around 13 kilometers west of town, south of Central Bedeque on Route 171, **Mid Isle Motel** (Rte. 171, 902/887-2525 or 877/877-2525, www.midisle.ca) offers 10 basic rooms for $60; a small adjacent café is open for breakfast.

❚ **Lord's Seaside Cottages** (Bells Point Rd. off Rte. 10, 902/437-2426 or 888/228-6765, www.lordsseasidecottages.com; June–Sept.; $100–130 s or d) is well worth the extra money. Sitting on Bells Point, a few kilometers west of Borden–Carleton, the eight simple cottages each have 1–3 bedrooms, a TV, and a deck with a barbecue. In June and September, you can rent any of the cottages for $550 per week—an excellent deal for families or two couples traveling together.

Charlottetown to Cavendish

The most direct route between Charlottetown and Cavendish is to take Route 2 west from the capital for 25 kilometers, then head north from Hunter River on Route 13. This drive takes less than one hour to reach the coast. A more leisurely alternative, and the one followed below, begins by taking Route 2 northeast from Charlottetown to Grand Tracadie and then following Route 6 east along the coast to Cavendish. If you've been traveling through Kings County (on Eastern Prince Edward Island), Tracadie Cross, the turnoff for the coastal route, is just seven kilometers west of Mount Stewart.

GRAND TRACADIE

Grand Tracadie is easily reached in around 40 minutes from Charlottetown. It is the eastern gateway to Prince Edward Island National Park but is best known for a historic inn that lies within the park, two kilometers from the town center.

Accommodations and Food

Elegant green-roofed ❚ **Dalvay by the Sea**

(16 Cottage Cres., 902/672-2048 or 888/366-2955, www.dalvaybythesea.com; mid-June–early Oct.) appeals to guests who like an old-money ambience. The rustic mansion was built in 1895 by millionaire American oil industrialist Alexander MacDonald, who used the lodging as a summer retreat. Today the hotel, its antiques, and its spacious grounds are painstakingly maintained by the national park staff. Its 26 rooms rent for $180–200 s, $280–380 d, including breakfast and dinner. Four cottages on the grounds ($470–510 d including meals) are most popular with honeymooners.

The hotel's dining room is locally renowned, and nonguests are welcome with advance reservations. Entrées ($20–36) feature formal Canadian cuisine prepared with a French flair. The emphasis is on the freshest produce, best seafood, and finest beef cuts. Mains include a rack of lamb crusted with hazelnut and grainy mustard; the sticky date pudding topped with toffee sauce is an easy choice for dessert. In July and August, a grand afternoon tea is served daily 2–4 P.M. for $20 per person (children pay $6 for cookies and lemonade). Other hotel facilities include a well-stocked gift shop, a nearby beach, a tennis court, bike rentals, a lake with canoes, and nature trails.

STANHOPE

From Grand Tracadie, there are two options for travelers heading west toward Cavendish: one along the coast within Prince Edward Island National Park, and the other through Stanhope.

Accommodations

Stanhope Bay and Beach Resort (3445 Bayshore Rd., 902/672-2701 or 866/672-2701, www.stanhopebeachresort.com; June–mid-Oct.; from $164 s or d) overlooks Covehead Bay and the national park from north of town. Dating to 1855, the resort has 86 units spread through numerous buildings. The resort recently underwent major renovations, with all rooms stylishly redecorated in decor that gives a contemporary feel to the Victorian style. Amenities include tennis, croquet, an outdoor

heated pool, bike and canoe rentals, and an adjacent golf course. Rates include a buffet-style breakfast and a discount on dinner.

BRACKLEY BEACH

With its proximity to the national park, excellent beaches, golf, deep-sea fishing, and other attractions, Brackley Beach is a popular base.

Just south of town is **Dunes Studio Gallery and Cafe** (Rte. 15, 902/672-2586; June–Oct. daily 10 A.M.–6 P.M.), an architecturally distinctive building with the ocean-facing wall composed almost entirely of windows. Inside, a wide spiral walkway passes the work of around 70 artists, including island craftspeople who create stoneware, framed photography, gold jewelry, pottery, watercolors, woodcarvings, oils, and sculptures. It's worth browsing just for porcelains crafted by owner Peter Jansons. Make sure you make your way up to the rooftop garden. For some of the island's most creative modern cooking, plan on enjoying lunch or dinner at the sunken rear of the gallery, in the café (June–Oct. daily 11:30 A.M.–10 P.M.) overlooking the gardens. You'll need reservations for dinner on weekends.

Accommodations and Camping

Distinctive red and white C **Shaw's Hotel** (99 Apple Tree Rd., 902/672-2022, www.shawshotel.ca) overlooks the bay from a 30-hectare peninsula at the edge of Prince Edward Island National Park. This was the Shaw family's homestead in the 1860s, and it's still in the family, now protected as a National Historic Site. The property has 16 antique-furnished guest rooms in the main house, 25 adjacent historic cottages, and 15 newer upscale waterfront chalets. Rates start at $145 s or d for a room only, or you can pay from $115 per person to include breakfast and dinner. The ambience is informal and friendly—a nice place for meeting islanders and other visitors. The dining room at Shaw's Hotel is consistently good; start with a chowder appetizer and stick to the chef's daily choices, prepared from whatever seafood is in season ($22–28).

Camping is available nearby at the

12-hectare **Vacationland Travel Park** (east of Rte. 15 overlooking Brackley Bay, 902/672-2317 or 800/529-0066, www.vacationlan-drv.pe.ca; mid-May–mid-Sept.; $29–43). Facilities include a dump station, store, canteen, Laundromat, heated pool, hot showers, mini-golf, and other recreational activities.

◖ PRINCE EDWARD ISLAND NATIONAL PARK

Prince Edward Island National Park's sandy beaches, dunes, sandstone cliffs, marshes, and forestlands represent Prince Edward Island as it once was, unspoiled by the crush of 20th-century development.

The park protects a slender 40-kilometer-long coastal slice of natural perfection, extending almost the full length of Queens County, as well as a six-square-kilometer spit of land farther east near Greenwich on the North Shore on eastern Prince Edward Island. The park also extends inland at Cavendish to include Green Gables House and Green Gables Golf Course. The main body of the park is book-ended by two large bays. At the eastern end, Tracadie Bay spreads out like an oversize pond with shimmering waters. Forty kilometers to the west, New London Bay forms almost a mirror image of the eastern end. In between, long barrier islands define Rustico and Covehead Bays, and sand dunes webbed with marram grass, rushes, fragrant bayberry, and wild roses front the coastline.

Sunrise and sunset here are cast in glowing colors. All along the gulf at sunrise, the beaches have a sense of primeval peacefulness, their sands textured like herringbone by the overnight sea breezes.

Getting around is easy. Route 6 lies on the park's inland side, connecting numerous park entrances, and the Gulf Shore Parkway runs along the coast nearly the park's entire length. You can drive through the park year-round. Cyclists will appreciate the smooth wide shoulders and light traffic along the Gulf Shore Parkway, which runs most of the length of the park.

Park Entry

Between early June and mid-September, the entrance fee for a one-day pass is adult $8, senior $7, child $4, to a maximum of $16 per vehicle. (The park entry fee does not apply for Green Gables House but is collected from those staying at park campgrounds).

Environmental Factors

The national park was established in 1937 to protect the fragile dunes along the Gulf of St. Lawrence and cultural features such as Green Gables House. Parks Canada walks a fine line, balancing environmental concerns with the responsibilities of hosting half a million park visitors a year. Boardwalks route visitors through dunes to the beaches and preserve the fragile landscape.

Bird-watchers will be amply rewarded with sightings of some of the more than 100 species known to frequent the park. Brackley Marsh, Orby Head, and the Rustico Island Causeway are good places to start. The park preserves nesting habitat for some 25 pairs of endangered piping plovers—small, shy shorebirds that arrive in early April to breed in flat sandy areas near the high-tide line. Some beaches may be closed in spring and summer when the plovers are nesting; it's vital to the birds' survival that visitors stay clear of these areas.

Recreation

The unbroken stretches of sandy beaches—some white, others tinted pink by iron oxide—are among the best in Atlantic Canada. On warm summer days, droves of sunbathers laze on the shore and swim in the usually gentle surf. The busier beaches have a lifeguard on duty, but always be aware of undertows.

Stanhope Beach, opposite the campground, is wide and flat, and remains relatively busy throughout summer. Next up to the east, **Brackley Beach** is backed by higher sand dunes. The adjacent visitor center has changing rooms and a snack bar. **Cavendish Beach** is the busiest of all; those toward Orby Head are backed by steep red-sandstone cliffs.

Established **hiking trails** range from the

0.5-kilometer wheelchair-accessible Reeds and Rushes Trail, beginning at the Dalvay Administration Building near Grand Tracadie, to the eight-kilometer Homestead Trail beginning near the entrance to Cavendish Campground. The latter wends inland alongside freshwater ponds and through woods and marshes and is open to both hikers and bikers. Be wary of potentially hazardous cliff edges, and of the poison ivy and ticks that lurk in the ground cover.

If you'd like to learn more about the park's ecology, join one of the **nature walks** led by Parks Canada rangers. The treks lead through white spruce stunted by winter storms and winds, to freshwater ponds, and into the habitats of such native animal species as red fox, northern phalarope, Swainson's thrush, and junco.

Campgrounds

The park's three campgrounds are distinctly different from one another. A percentage of sites can be reserved through the **Parks Canada Campground Reservation Service** (905/426-4648 or 877/737-3783, www.pccamping.ca) for $11 per reservation. During July and August and especially for weekends, reservations are recommended. The remaining sites are sold on a first-come, first-served basis.

Stanhope Campground (north of Stanhope; mid-June–early Oct.) is across the road from the ocean and has 95 unserviced sites ($25.50), 16 sites with two-way hookups ($32), and 14 sites with full hookups ($36). Amenities include showers, a playground, a grocery store, laundry facilities, and wooded tent sites.

Closest to Cavendish and center of the park's summer interpretive program is **Cavendish Campground** (late May–early Oct.). This, the most popular of the three campgrounds, has 230 unserviced sites ($25.50) and 78 hookup sites ($34–36). Campground facilities include a grocery store, kitchen shelters, launderettes, flush toilets, and hot showers.

Information

The main **Cavendish Visitor Centre** is combined with the provincially operated Visitor Information Centre, 50 meters north of the Route 6 and Route 13 intersection in Cavendish (902/963-2391; mid-May–mid-Oct. daily 9 A.M.–5 P.M., July–Aug. daily 8 A.M.–10 P.M.). As well as general park information, displays depict the park's natural history, and a small shop sells park-related literature and souvenirs. Another source of information is the website www.pc.gc.ca.

RUSTICO BAY

A decade after the French began Port-la-Joye near Charlottetown, French settlers cut through the inland forest and settled Rustico Bay's coastline. England's Acadian deportation in 1755 emptied the villages, but not for long. The Acadians returned, and the five revived Rusticos—Rusticoville, Rustico, Anglo Rustico, North Rustico, and North Rustico Harbour—still thrive and encircle Rustico Bay's western shore.

Sights

For a glimpse at Acadian culture, check out the imposing two-story **Farmers' Bank of Rustico Museum** (Church Rd., Rustico, 902/963-3168; mid-June–Sept. Mon.–Sat. 9:30 A.M.–5:30 P.M., Sun. 1–5:30 P.M.; adult $4). Built in 1864 as Canada's first chartered people's bank (the precursor of today's credit unions), the building served as the early Acadian banking connection, then as a library. Exhibits at this national historic site include heritage displays plus artifacts from the life of the Reverend Georges-Antoine Belcourt, the founder.

Accommodations and Camping

Accommodations at **Rustico Resort** (corner Rte. 6 and Rte. 242, Rustico, 902/963-2357, www.rusticoresort.com; May–Oct.) are usually filled with golfers, who stay in the cottages for $175 s or d, including breakfast and unlimited golf on the adjacent course. Other amenities include grass tennis courts, a heated pool, and a dining room with a lounge.

The 1870 **Barachois Inn** (2193 Church Rd., Rustico, 902/963-2194, www.barachoisinn.com;

May–Oct.; $160–200 s or d) overlooks Rustico Bay from just off Route 243. The main house holds four historically themed guest rooms while the adjacent McDonald House contains four larger, more modern rooms. Rates include a full breakfast.

Cymbria Tent and Trailer Park (Rte. 242, Cambria, 902/963-2458, www.cymbria.ca; mid-May–mid-Oct.) occupies a quiet 12-hectare location close to the beach four kilometers east of Rustico. Campsites are $26 unserviced, $30–35 with hookups. Facilities include a store, game room, playground, dump station, and hot showers.

Food

Fisherman's Wharf Lobster Suppers (Rte. 6, North Rustico, 902/963-2669; June–mid-Oct. daily 11 A.M.–9 P.M.) is a cavernous 400-seat restaurant that attracts the tour bus crowd from Cavendish. Choose from three different sizes of lobster ($30–38), pay your money, and join the fray. The cost includes one full lobster and unlimited trips to the buffet counter, including chowder, mussels, hot entrées, salad, dessert, and hot drinks.

If your accommodation has cooking facilities, head to **Doiron Fisheries** (North Rustico dock, 902/963-2442; May–early Oct. daily 8 A.M.–8 P.M.) for lobsters, mussels, clams, fish, and delicious Malpeque Bay oysters.

🄲 NORTH RUSTICO HARBOUR

This tiny village on the north side of Rustico Bay is one of my favorite spots on Prince Edward Island. It slopes down to the water, where you find a restored wharf with an interesting interpretive center, fishing charters, and sea-kayak rentals. Add to the scene an old wooden lighthouse and one of the region's best restaurants, and you have a destination as far removed from nearby commercial Cavendish as you could imagine.

Sights and Recreation

While you should make sure to wander along the wharf and beyond the lighthouse to North

the lighthouse at North Rustico Harbour

Rustico Beach (which is within Prince Edward Island National Park), there is also **Rustico Harbour Fishery Museum** (318 Harbourview Dr., 902/963-3799; mid-May–Sept. daily 9:30 A.M.–5:30 P.M.; adult $4, child $2). This small well-designed facility, sitting on the main wharf, centers around a lobster-fishing boat. Displays tell the story of the Mi'Kmaq who lived across the bay on Robinsons Island for 1,500 years and also chronicle fishing since the arrival of Europeans.

Half a dozen charter fishing operators tie up at North Rustico Harbour. The average cost is a remarkably low $30 per person for a three-hour outing or $150 for a full day's charter, for cod, mackerel, flounder, and tuna. Most charters operate July to mid-September. The crew will outfit you in raingear if needed, provide tackle and bait, and clean and fillet your catch. **Aiden's Deep-sea Fishing** (902/963-3522) has been in business for decades and has three excursions scheduled daily.

North Rustico Harbour is the push-off point for kayak tours operated by **Outside**

Expeditions (902/963-3366; mid-May–mid-Oct.). A 90-minute paddle around the bay is $39 per person; a three-hour trip, with the chance of seeing abundant bird life, is $50; and a six hour trip across to Robinsons Island is $100 including lunch.

Food

A shack on the main dock has been converted to the **Blue Mussel Café** (Harbourview Dr., 902/963-2152; mid-June–mid-Sept. daily 11:30 A.M.–8 P.M.), a tiny little restaurant where most of the tables are outside on a private corner of the wharf. The menu reads like a list of what fisherfolk haul in from local waters—salmon, haddock, mussels, lobster—and unlike at most other island restaurants, there's not a deep fryer in sight.

Cavendish

Thanks to Lucy Maud Montgomery and a certain fictional character named Anne, Cavendish, 40 kilometers northeast of Charlottetown, is Prince Edward Island's most popular tourist destination. Unfortunately, those who come here expecting to find a bucolic little oasis of tranquility will be sorely disappointed. The once rural Cavendish area has become a maze of theme parks, fast-food outlets, and souvenir shops in parts, and the village has repositioned itself as an official resort municipality to try to grapple with fame. To dedicated readers of Montgomery's sentimental books, the village's lure is emotional. For others—those who don't know Anne of Green Gables from Anne Frank—it might best be avoided. Still, if you end up here and are looking for something to do, you'll have a multitude of choices—including heading into adjacent Prince Edward Island National Park, golfing at Green Gables Golf Course, or browsing through crafts shops.

© ANDREW HEMPSTEAD

Green Gables House is the most popular of many "Anne attractions" in and around Cavendish.

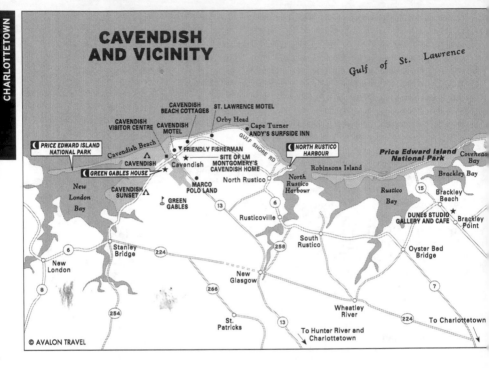

CAVENDISH AND VICINITY

© AVALON TRAVEL

UTOPIAN AVONLEA

Montgomery portrayed rural Cavendish as an idyllic "never land" called Avonlea, imbued with innocence and harmony. Beyond the crass commercialism, as you drive the rambling red-clay lanes and walk the quiet woods, meadows, and gulf shore, you'll have to agree the lady did not overstate her case. The most pastoral and historic places are preserved as part of **Prince Edward Island National Park.** Cavendish itself is home to two important Anne attractions, while others dot the surrounding countryside.

【 Green Gables House

Located on the west side of the Route 6 and Route 13 intersection, Green Gables House (902/963-7874; May–Oct. daily 9 A.M.–5 P.M., July–Aug. until 6 P.M.; adult $8, senior $7, child $4) reigns as the idyllic hub of a Montgomery sightseeing circuit. The restored 19th-century farmhouse, once home of Montgomery's elderly cousins and the setting for her most famous book, *Anne of Green Gables,* is furnished simply and stolidly, just as it was described in the novel. A fire in 1997 badly damaged portions of the house, but repairs commenced immediately, and within a couple of weeks the landmark was back in perfect condition. Among other memorabilia in the pretty vintage setting are artifacts such as the author's archaic typewriter, on which she composed so many well-loved passages. Period-style gardens, farm buildings, and an interpretive center and gift shop complete the complex. Also on the grounds, the Balsam Hollow and Haunted Woods trails feature some of Montgomery's favorite woodland haunts, including Lover's Lane.

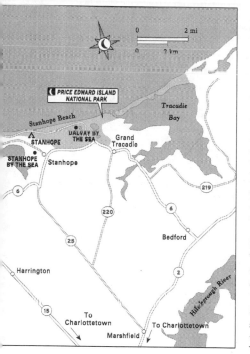

Site of Lucy Maud Montgomery's Cavendish Home

Montgomery spent much of her childhood living with her grandparents in a small home one kilometer east of Green Gables House. "I wrote it in the evenings after my regular day's work was done," she recalled, "wrote most of it at the window of the little gable room that had been mine for many years." While the main building is long gone, the stone cellar remains. Surrounded by a white picket fence and by apple trees, it has been converted to a small museum and bookstore (Rte. 6, 902/963-2231; mid-May–mid-Oct. daily 9 A.M.–5 P.M., July–Aug. daily 9 A.M.–6 P.M.; adult $3, child $1) operated by Montgomery's descendants.

Montgomery is buried behind the adjacent United Church.

RECREATION
Golf

Little known outside Canada, Stanley Thompson was one of the world's great golf course architects of the mid-20th century. His best-known courses were those within the country's national park system. **Green Gables Golf Course** (Rte. 6, 902/963-4653) may not be as revered as Thompson-designed Highland Links (Cape Breton Highlands National Park) or Banff Springs (Banff National Park), but this old-fashioned layout within Prince Edward Island National Park is a gem of composition defined by water views and deep bunkers. Regular greens fees are $100 including a cart, or pay $55 after 3 P.M.

Fun Parks

The only theme park with any relationship to Anne of Green Gables is **Avonlea** (Rte. 6, 902/963-3050; mid-June–Sept. daily 10 A.M.–5 P.M.; adult $20, senior $18, child $16). Staff in period costumes bring the life and times of Anne to life in musical shows that take place throughout the sprawling grounds. Visitors are invited to try their hand at milking a cow, learn how to barn dance, and tour an old-fashioned chocolate factory.

You'll see the rides of **Sandspit** amusement park (Rte. 6, 902/963-2626; last week of June daily 10 A.M.–6 P.M., July–early Sept. daily 10 A.M.–11 P.M.), east of the junction of Routes 6 and 13, long before arriving at the front gate. The huge park, a magnet for kids on vacation, features a roller coaster (The Cyclone—billed as the largest in the Maritimes), a carousel, and other rides, rides, rides. It's free to get in, but each ride costs a small amount. All-day ride packages cost $12–22, depending on your height.

And what tourist town would be complete without a **Ripley's Believe It or Not! Museum** (Cranberry Village, Rte. 6, 902/963-2242; June and Sept. daily 9:30 A.M.–5:30 P.M., July–Aug. daily 9 A.M.–10 P.M.; adult $9, senior $7, child $5.50) or a wax museum—in this case the

LUCY MAUD MONTGOMERY

Lucy Maud Montgomery, known and beloved around the world as the creator of *Anne of Green Gables,* was born at New London, Prince Edward Island, in 1874, a decade after the Charlottetown Conference. When Lucy was only two, her mother died and her father moved to western Canada. Maud, as she preferred to be called, was left in the care of her maternal grandparents, who brought her to Cavendish.

Cavendish, in northern Queens County, was idyllic in those days, and Montgomery wrote fondly about the ornate Victorian sweetness of the setting of her early years. As a young woman, she studied first at the island's Prince of Wales College, later at Dalhousie University in Halifax. She then returned to the island as a teacher at Bideford, Lower Bedeque, Belmont, and Lot 15. In 1898 her grandfather's death brought her back to Cavendish to help her grandmother.

The idea for *Anne of Green Gables* dated to the second Cavendish stay, and the book was published in 1908. In 1911, Montgomery married the Rev. Ewen MacDonald at her Campbell relatives' Silver Bush homestead overlooking the Lake of Shining Waters. (The Campbell descendants still live in the pretty farmhouse and have turned their home into a museum.) The couple moved to Ontario, where Montgomery spent the rest of her life, returning to PEI only for short visits. Although she left, Maud never forgot Prince Edward Island. Those brief revisitations with her beloved is-land must have been painful; after one trip, she wistfully recalled in her journal:

This evening I spent in Lover's Lane. How beautiful it was – green and alluring and beckoning! I had been tired and discouraged and sick at heart before I went to it – and it rested me and cheered me and stole away the heartsickness, giving peace and newness of life.

Montgomery died in 1942 and was buried in Cavendish Cemetery. As an author, she left 20 juvenile books and myriad other writings. Her works have been published worldwide, translated into 16 languages. In Japan, Montgomery's writings are required reading in the school system – which accounts for the island's many Japanese visitors.

Montgomery wrote for children, and she viewed Cavendish and Prince Edward Island with all the clarity and innocence that a child possesses. Her books are as timeless today as they were decades ago. Some critics have described Montgomery's writings as mawkish. Contemporary scholars, however, have taken a new look at the author's works and have begun to discern a far more complex style. The academic community may debate her literary prowess, but no matter – the honest essence of Montgomery's writings has inspired decades of zealous pilgrims to pay their respects to her native Cavendish. To islanders, she is Lucy Maud, their literary genius, on a first-name basis.

adjacent **Wax World of the Stars** (Cranberry Village, Rte. 6, 902/963-2350), which has a similar admission price and hours.

FESTIVALS AND EVENTS

Lucy Maud Montgomery Festival is a summer-long gathering (www.lmmontgomery-festival.com) that attracts Anne fans from around the world. Children especially will be enchanted by a schedule of events that includes re-creations of various events in Montgomery's life, a coloring competition in the local school-house, Victorian-era lawn games, writing workshops, and an ice-cream picnic. Parents are catered to with book readings and carriage rides, and, of course, they are also invited to the ice-cream picnic.

ACCOMMODATIONS AND CAMPING

While accommodations in Cavendish are plentiful, they book up well in advance for July and August. No place in Atlantic Canada sees a more dramatic drop in room rates for the shoulder seasons (mid-May–June and Sept.–mid-Oct.), while the rest of the year most accommodations close completely.

Under $50
⬤ Andy's Surfside Inn (Gulf Shore Rd., 902/963-2405; June–Nov.; $45–75 s or d) is a big old whitewashed home right on the ocean a few kilometers east of Cavendish along the coastal road. The rooms and facilities are older, but the setting can't be beat. Only one room has its own bathroom; other amenities include a deck, bikes, and a barbecue.

$50-100
The **St. Lawrence Motel** (351 Gulf Shore Rd., 902/963-2053 or 800/387-2053, www.stlawrencemotel.com; mid-May–Sept.; $69–159 s or d) is within Prince Edward Island National Park between Cavendish and North Rustico. Set on eight hectares, this 16-room property overlooks the gulf a short walk from the water.

All but one of the units has a kitchen, and the largest have three bedrooms. The beach is a short walk down the road and on-site amenities include a recreation room, barbecues, and lawn games such as horseshoes and croquet. Rates include free park entry.

Silverwood Motel (Rte. 6, 902/963-2439 or 800/565-4753, www.silverwoodmotel.com; mid-May–mid-Oct.) has regular motel rooms for $94 s or d, one-bedroom units with kitchens for $114 s or d, and two-bedroom kitchen-equipped units for $144 s or d. There's also a pool and adjacent restaurant.

Cavendish Motel (corner Rte. 6 and Rte. 13, 902/963-2244 or 800/565-2243, www.cavendishmotel.pe.ca; May–Oct.; from 115 s or d) offers a mix of regularly revamped rooms with surprises such as big 27-inch TVs. Amenities include barbecues, a heated pool, a dining room, and a playground.

Over $100
From **⬤ Kindred Spirits Country Inn and Cottages** (Memory Ln., off Rte. 6, 902/963-2434

© ANDREW HEMPSTEAD

Kindred Spirits Country Inn and Cottages

or 800/461-1755, www.kindredspirits.ca; mid-May–mid-Oct.), guests can stroll along Lover's Lane to Green Gables House, just the way Lucy Maud Montgomery described in *Anne of Green Gables*. This grandly Victorian estate is also handy to the golf course, but also very private and far removed from busy Route 6. Bed-and-breakfast rooms in the main inn ($135–180 s or d) are decorated with stylish antiques. Some have balconies and fireplaces. Surrounding the inn are 14 kitchen-equipped cottages, each surrounded by green space. Rates range from $205 for a one-bedroom unit to $375 for a three-bedroom cottage with a whirlpool bath.

Overlooking the Gulf of St. Lawrence from within Prince Edward Island National Park is **Cavendish Beach Cottages** (Gulf Shore Rd., 902/963-2025, www.cavendishbeachcottages .com; early May–mid-Oct.; $155–209 s or d), a complex of 13 simply furnished yet modern cottages, each with a deck offering ocean views. The cottages, set back 200 meters from the beach, are just a few steps from the park's jogging and hiking trails. Off-season rates (late May and early October) start at $90.

Campgrounds

What (**Cavendish Campground** (late May–early Oct.; $24–38) lacks in facilities it makes up for in location, close to the ocean within Prince Edward Island National Park and just a few kilometers from downtown Cavendish. Amenities include showers, kitchen shelters, and fire pits (firewood $8 per bundle). Even with over 300 campsites, it fills most summer days, so plan on arriving before noon or booking a site in advance. These can be made through the **Parks Canada Campground Reservation Service** (905/426-4648 or 877/737-3783, www.pccamping.ca) for $11 per reservation.

Marco Polo Land (Rte. 13, 902/963-2352 or 800/665-2352, www.marcopololand.com; late May–mid-Oct.; $28–42) is the island's definitive commercial campground, replete with resort trappings. Facilities at the 40-hectare park

include over 400 campsites ($24–31), tennis courts, mini-golf, a full-sized outdoor pool, a wading pool, a restaurant, a campers' store, a Laundromat, and hot showers.

The 465-site **Cavendish Sunset Campground** (Rte. 6, 902/963-2440 or 800/715-2440, www.cavendishsunsetcampground.com; mid-June–early Sept.; $30–38) is big, bold, and very family-friendly. It has all the amenities of Marco Polo Land except the restaurant.

FOOD
Lobster Supper

Lobster suppers are casual good-value gatherings held across the island. They can be very commercial or simply an annual gathering of locals in a church basement. A great compromise is the (**New Glasgow Lobster Supper** (Rte. 258, 902/964-2870; June–mid-Oct. 4–8:30 P.M.), eight kilometers southeast of Cavendish along Route 13. In operation since 1958, this one fills the local community hall with up to 500 diners at a time. It even has its own lobster holding pond, allowing the tradition to continue beyond lobster-fishing season. Choose the size of lobster (between one and two pounds) and then have it boiled up while you feast on a buffet of mussels, clam chowder, salad, breads, and nonalcoholic drinks for a set price ($30–42 per person).

Other Dining Options

One cannot live on lobster alone, so if you're in town more than one night, you'll need to find somewhere else to eat once you've participated in a lobster supper. The best restaurant in the region is the (**Blue Mussel Café** (Harbourview Dr., 902/963-2152; mid-June–mid-Sept. daily 11:30 A.M.–8 P.M.), six kilometers east at North Rustico Harbour, or if you have cooking facilities at your accommodation (even just a barbecue), pick up fresh seafood at **Doiron Fisheries** (North Rustico dock, 902/963-2442; May–early Oct. daily 8 A.M.–8 P.M.).

In Cavendish itself, most restaurants are

family-style and very touristy—great if you have children, but that's about it. The most popular of these is the **Friendly Fisherman** (corner Rte. 6 and Rte. 13, 902/963-2234; mid-June–mid-Oct. daily 8 A.M.–8 P.M.). It advertises very cheap breakfasts, but the crowds come mainly for dinner buffets. Adult pay from $15 and children pay $2 per year of their age.

For do-it-yourself meals, take your choice of markets along major highways; shops at **Cavendish Beach Shopping Plaza** answer most needs. The main excuse to stop at **Cavendish Boardwalk,** another mall, is for an ice cream at **Cow's** (902/963-2692).

INFORMATION AND SERVICES

Cavendish has no downtown. Instead, services such as restaurants and gas stations are scattered along a five-kilometer stretch of Route 6 southeast from the junction with Route 13. For chores such as grocery shopping, banking, and posting mail, plan on doing that back in Charlottetown.

The provincial **Visitor Information Centre** (corner Rte. 6 and Rte. 13, 902/963-7830; June and Sept. daily 9 A.M.–5 P.M., July–Aug. daily 9 A.M.–8 P.M.) represents local operators and accommodations. Tourism Prince Edward Island shares the building with Parks Canada (902/963-2391), which hands out park information.

VICINITY OF CAVENDISH

Hamlets encircle Cavendish. The rural scenery is lovely, and exploring the beaches and back roads should help you sharpen your appetite for a night at one of PEI's famed lobster-supper community halls, which are scattered hereabouts.

Stanley Bridge

For seaworthy sightseeing, check out **Stanley Bridge Marine Aquarium** (Rte. 6, 902/886-3355; mid-June–Sept. daily 9:30 A.M.–8 P.M.; adult $7.50, child $4.50), five kilometers

southwest of Cavendish. The privately operated aquarium has native fish species in viewing tanks and exhibits on natural history and oyster cultivation; seals are kept outside in penned pools. Part of the complex is an oyster bar with a deck built over the water.

In the vicinity, shoppers like the **Stanley Bridge Studios** (Rte. 6, 902/886-2800), where shelves and floor space overflow with woolen sweaters, quilts, apparel, stoneware, porcelain, jewelry, and Anne dolls. **Old Stanley Schoolhouse** (corner Rte. 6 and Rte. 224, 902/886-2033) handles island-made quilts, weaving, pottery, pewter, folk art, and sweaters.

New London

The **Lucy Maud Montgomery Birthplace** (corner Rte. 6 and Rte. 20, 902/886-2099; mid-May–Oct. daily 9 A.M.–5 P.M.; adult $3, child $1) lies 10 minutes from Cavendish at what was once Clifton. The author was born in the unassuming house in 1874. The exhib its include her wedding dress, scrapbooks, and other personal items.

Old-fashioned tea rooms dot the countryside around Cavendish, and none are more welcoming than **◖ Blue Winds Tea House** (10746 New London Rd., 902/886-2860; Fri.–Wed. 11:30 A.M.–6 P.M., Thurs. 2–5 P.M.), on the south side of the village. Here, the soups are made from scratch, breads and pastries are baked daily, and recipes for treats such as New Moon Pudding are taken from historic cookbooks. On Thursday, afternoon tea is served for $11 per person.

Park Corner

Anne of Green Gables Museum (Rte. 20, 902/436-7329; May–Oct. daily 11 A.M.–4 P.M., summer 9 A.M.–4 P.M.; adult $3, child $1), eight kilometers northwest of New London, is another Montgomery landmark and the ancestral home of the author's Campbell relatives. The estate spreads out in a farmhouse setting in the pastoral rolling countryside, with the Lake of Shining

Waters, described in *Anne of Green Lakes,* in front of the main buildings. Montgomery described the house as "the big beautiful home that was the wonder castle of my dreams," and here she was married in 1911. The museum's exhibits include Montgomery's personal correspondence and first editions of her works.

The adjacent **Shining Waters Tea Room** (902/886-2003) serves island-style light fare, and the crafts shop sells Montgomery souvenirs as well as wind chimes, quilts, and other crafts.

PRINCE COUNTY

Prince County encompasses the western third of Prince Edward Island. Like Kings County in the east, it is well off the main tourist path. Along the southern portion of Prince County, the land is level, and the pastoral farmlands flow in gentle serene sweeps to the strait coastline. Thick woodlands span the county's midsection, and you'll see fields of potatoes that blossom in July and green carpets of wheat nodding in the summer breezes. The northern tip is a remote and barren plain with a windswept coast, where farmers known as "mossers" use stout draft horses to reap Irish moss (a seaweed) from the surf.

Summerside, the province's second-largest town, boasts an ample supply of lodgings, restaurants, and nightlife. Just west of there is the province's largest Acadian area, the Région Évangéline. Count on high-quality crafts and wares at town boutiques and outlying shops throughout the region; the region's craftspeople are renowned for quilts, knitted apparel, Acadian shirts, and blankets.

Route 2, PEI's main expressway, enters Prince County at the town of Kensington, glides past the seaport of Summerside on a narrow isthmus, and leads inland for 100 kilometers to finish at the village of Tignish, near the island's northwestern tip. The highways up and down the east and west coasts come together to be known as Lady Slipper Scenic Drive, one of the provincial scenic sightseeing routes (it's signposted with a red symbol of the orchidlike flower). The county's most idyllic scenery—and some of the island's most spectacular sea views—lie along this route, at the sea's edges

© ANDREW HEMPSTEAD

PRINCE COUNTY

HIGHLIGHTS

◖ **College of Piping:** Students from around the world gather at this school to learn the art of bagpiping and highland dancing, and visitors are more than welcome to watch (page 42).

◖ **Tyne Valley:** A gem of composition, this small village straddling the Tyne River comprises neat homes, arts and crafts shops, and an inviting lodge (page 44).

◖ **Green Park Shipbuilding Museum and Yeo House:** An attraction that is as scenic as it is historic, this waterfront estate was once the center of a thriving shipbuilding industry (page 45).

◖ **Our Lady of Mont-Carmel Acadian Church:** This magnificent church rises high above the trim Acadian homes of Mont-Carmel (page 47).

◖ **Prince Edward Island Potato Museum:** Learn about the province's main agricultural crop at this museum; it is more interesting than the name might suggest (page 49).

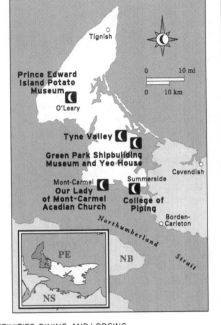

LOOK FOR ◖ TO FIND RECOMMENDED SIGHTS, ACTIVITIES, DINING, AND LODGING.

of Northumberland Strait and the Gulf of St. Lawrence. Around 50 meandering side roads lead off the coastal route to connect with Route 2 and others. You may become temporarily lost on the roads, but not for long—the blue sea invariably looms around the next bend.

PLANNING YOUR TIME

It's possible to reach the northern tip of Prince County on a day trip from Charlottetown, but a more sensible option if you have just one day would be to concentrate on the southern half of the county. A suggested route would be to stop in Summerside to visit the **College of Piping,** drive through Région Évangéline past the spectacular **Our Lady of Mont-Carmel Acadian Church,** and jog north to picturesque **Tyne Valley** and the nearby **Green Park Shipbuilding Museum**

and Yeo House. The main reason to explore further is for the coastal scenery, especially along the Northumberland Strait. Other attractions include the **Prince Edward Island Potato Museum,** golfing at Mill River, and the feeling of accomplishment of driving to the end of the road at North Cape.

Tourist services are more limited in Prince County than elsewhere in the province. You should be able to find somewhere to stay with a few days' notice, but for top picks such as **West Point Lighthouse** (West Point) and **Doctor's Inn** (Tyne Valley), plan on being disappointed if you arrive without reservations. You won't need reservations at my favorite two Prince County eateries—**Flex Mussels** (Summerside) and the **Seaweed Pie Café** (Miminegash)—but you will need a sense of adventure for the latter.

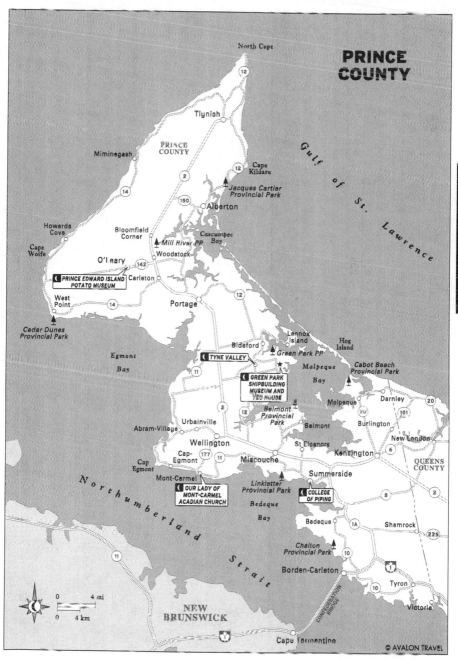

PRINCE COUNTY

Summerside

Summerside (pop. 17,000), 72 kilometers west of Charlottetown and 30 kilometers northwest of the Confederation Bridge, is Prince Edward Island's second-largest town and its main shipping port. It's got all the bustle yet none of the seaminess usually associated with seaports. Stately old homes anchor wide lawns, and quiet streets are edged with verdant canopies.

SIGHTS AND RECREATION
Along the Harbor

The tourist's Summerside lies along Harbour Drive, where **Spinnakers' Landing** was developed after a military base was phased out. The complex comprises numerous shops and restaurants, an outdoor stage built over the water, a nautical-themed playground, and a lighthouse.

Taking its name from the Mi'Kmaq word for hot spot, **Eptek Art & Cultural Centre** (130 Harbour Dr., 902/888-8373; July–Aug. Mon.–Sat. 9 A.M.–5 P.M., Sun. noon–5 P.M., the rest of the year Tues.–Sat. only; admission varies) has a spacious main gallery hosting touring national fine arts and historical exhibits.

Wyatt House Museum

The home of Wanda Lefurgey Wyatt until her death at 102 in 1998, this grandly restored 1867 home (85 Spring St., 902/432-1327; June–Sept. Mon.–Sat. 10 A.M.–5 P.M.; adult $5.50, child $4.50) allows you to step back into the lives of a well-to-do family with long ties to the Summerside community. Adding to the charm are guided tours led by costumed guides.

College of Piping

The College of Piping (619 Water St. E., 902/436-5377, www.collegeofpiping.com), affiliated with Scotland's College of Piping in Glasgow, attracts students from around the world to its teaching programs of highland dancing, step dancing, fiddling, and

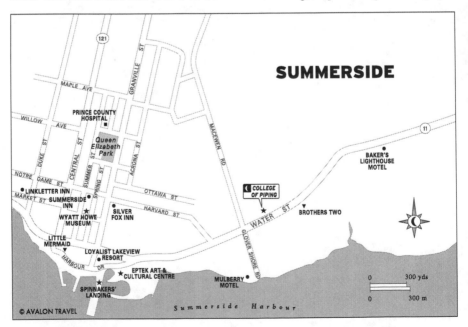

bagpiping. Students perform for the public at a series of summer concerts that take place daily at 11:30 A.M., 1:30 P.M., and 3:30 P.M. ($5 per person). Another program open to the public is the Highland Storm ceilidh (July–Aug. Tues.–Thurs. 7 P.M.; adult $24, senior $20, child $15). The college also offers short-term summer classes (about $25 per hour) in highland dancing, piping, and drumming. Check the website for a schedule.

ACCOMMODATIONS AND CAMPING
$50-100

Summerside's least expensive motel is **Baker's Lighthouse Motel** (802 Water St., 902/436-2992; $65 s, $75 d), two kilometers east of downtown. The rooms are plain but clean and comfortable. There's also a laundry and barbecues.

On the same side of town, but within walking distance of the waterfront, is the **Mulberry Motel** (6 Water St. E., 902/436-2520 or 800/274-3825). Each of the 13 guest rooms is spacious and has basic cooking facilities. On the downside, the televisions are very small, but for $75 s, $80 d, that's of little consequence.

Summerside Inn (98 Summer St., 902/436-1417 or 877/477-1417, www.summersideinn.net; $85–100 s or d) is a stately mansion three blocks from the harbor that has been converted to a bed-and-breakfast. The tasteful restoration has included stained-glass windows, hardwood floors, and period antiques. Four of the six guest rooms have en suite bathrooms with the remaining two sharing a single bathroom. Rates include a cooked breakfast.

$100-150

The 1890 Queen Anne Revival **C Silver Fox Inn** (61 Granville St., 902/436-1664 or 800/565-4033, www.silverfoxinn.net; $110–140 s or d) reigns locally as one of the seaport's "fox houses," built with a silver fox fortune and designed by architect William Critchlow Harris. The comfortable lodging has six guest rooms furnished with antiques and also with air-conditioning, TVs, and phones. With its

wing-backed chairs and shelves of reading material, the living area is a relaxing place to spend the evening.

The 108-room **Linkletter Inn** (311 Market St., 902/436-2157 or 800/565-7829; $120–170) is centrally located and offers large rooms (some with kitchenettes), a restaurant, a lounge, and amenities for the physically challenged.

Across the road from Spinnakers' Landing, **Loyalist Lakeview Resort** (195 Harbour Dr., 902/436-3333 or 800/361-2668, www.lakeviewhotels.com; $135–170 s or d) features 103 spacious motel rooms decorated with a distinct country inn–style decor. It offers a good range of amenities—tennis, an indoor pool, a fitness room, bike rentals, a pub, and a restaurant—making it a good choice for those looking for city-type accommodations.

Campground

Summerside's closest campground is in **Linkletter Provincial Park**, eight kilometers west of town (Rte. 11, 902/888-8366, mid June–mid-Sept.). This 30-hectare park on Bedeque Bay has 84 serviced and unserviced sites ($22–28), hot showers, a Laundromat, a dump station, a kitchen shelter, and a nearby store.

FOOD

Away from the water, **Brothers Two** (618 Water St. E., 902/436-9654; daily 11 A.M.–9:30 P.M.) has been Summerside's social hub for decades. It's no-frills family-style seafood dining at its best. Mains range $15–24 and come as simple as meatloaf and as fancy as scallops poached in white wine. If it's a warm evening, talk your way to a table on the rooftop patio.

INFORMATION

In the heart of harborfront Spinnakers' Landing, the **Visitor Information Centre** (Harbour Dr., 902/888-8364, www.city.summerside.pe.ca; late June–early Sept. daily 9:30 A.M.–9:30 P.M.) is well signposted as you come into town.

The **Rotary Regional Library** (192 Water St., 902/436-7323; Mon.–Fri. 10 A.M.–5 P.M.) has public Internet access.

Malpeque Bay

Sheltered from the open gulf by the long, narrow sandbar of Hog Island, the shallow waters of broad Malpeque Bay are tranquil and unpolluted. The bay's long fretted coastline is deserted, nearly bereft of development apart from three small provincial parks. Conditions are perfect for the large oyster fishery that thrives here. Ten million Malpeque oysters—Canada's largest source of the shellfish—are harvested each year. The purity of the bay water in part accounts for the excellent flavor of the oysters, which has made them famed worldwide as a gustatory treat. You'll find them served in a variety of ways at restaurants in the region.

KENSINGTON

Kensington lies at the intersection of five roads, including the trans-island Route 2. Summerside is 15 kilometers to the southwest, Charlottetown is 48 kilometers to the east, and Cavendish is 38 kilometers to the northeast.

Sights

Make your first stop **Kensington Railyards,** where you'll find the **Welcome Centre** (902/836-3031 or 877/836-3031, www.kata.pe.ca; May–Oct. daily 9 A.M.–9 P.M.) and a **farmers market** (July–Sept. Sat. 10 A.M.–2 P.M.), a good place to come for fresh produce, baked goods, snacks, and crafts.

On the main road through town, **Kensington Water Gardens** (Rte. 2, 902/836-3336; mid-June and Sept. daily 10 A.M.–5 P.M., July–Aug. daily 9 A.M.–7 P.M.; adult $6, child $3) is a popular spot with children. It features Tudor-style castles large and small, and kid-friendly water attractions.

CABOT BEACH PROVINCIAL PARK

From Kensington, Route 2 loops around the head of Malpeque Bay to the Tyne Valley, but Cabot Beach Provincial Park is worth a short detour (10 minutes).

This 140-hectare park (902/836-8945; late June–early Sept.), 30 kilometers north of Summerside on Route 105, is the most worthwhile attraction along the east side of Malpeque Bay. It occupies a gorgeous setting on a peninsula tip just inside the bay, including a coastline of sandy beaches broken by rocky headlands. At the park's day-use area is **Fanning School** (mid-June–mid-Sept. daily 10 A.M.–dusk; free), a schoolhouse built in 1794 and unique (for the time) for having two stories. Finally closed in 1969, it's now open to the public. Facilities at the park campground include over 150 sites (unserviced sites $22, hookups $25–28), a supervised ocean beach, a launderette, hot showers, kitchen shelters, and a nearby campers' store.

◖ TYNE VALLEY

Quiet and bucolic, the crossroads hamlet of Tyne Valley (pop. 200), at the intersection of backcountry Routes 12, 178, and 167, lies on the west side of Malpeque Bay, a 50-minute drive from Summerside and uncountable kilometers from the rest of the modern world.

In the 1800s, Tyne Valley began as a Green Park suburb. Two generations of the Yeo family dominated the island's economy with their shipbuilding yards on Malpeque Bay, and the empire begun by James Yeo—the feisty, entrepreneurial English merchant who arrived in the 1830s—spawned the next generation's landed gentry.

The empire's riches are gone, but the lovely landscape remains, like a slice of Lucy Maud Montgomery's utopian Avonlea, transplanted from Cavendish to this corner of Prince County. To get there, follow Route 12 around Malpeque Bay, or from Route 2, turn east on Route 132 or 133. The paved and red-clay roads ripple across the farmlands like velvet ribbons on plump quilts.

The quiet village stirs to life on the first weekend of August with the **Tyne Valley Oyster Festival,** a three-day tribute to

Malpeque oysters. Daytime oyster-farming exhibits and evening oyster and lobster dinners are accompanied by talent shows, oyster-shucking demonstrations, fiddling and step-dancing contests, a parade, and a dance.

Accommodations and Food

€ **Doctor's Inn** (Rte. 167, 902/831-3057; $55 s, $70 d) belonged to the village doctor during the late 1800s, and the inn's luster still sparkles, polished by innkeepers Jean and Paul Offer, who lovingly tend to almost one hectare of vegetable and fruit gardens. The inn has a formal front entrance, but everyone arrives at the side kitchen door and enters the busy kitchen fray, as the Offers process, can, and preserve the backyard's produce. Beyond the door to the dining room, the inn's interior gleams with antiques. A four-course dinner is served with advance reservations ($45 per person with wine) in the elegant, spacious dining room. Upstairs are three welcoming guest rooms.

VICINITY OF TYNE VALLEY
Green Park Provincial Park

Take Route 12 northeast from Tyne Valley and continue north through the hamlet of Port Hill to reach this beautiful park, protecting a peninsula that juts into Malpeque Bay. From the end of the road (at the Shipbuilding Museum), a three-kilometer hiking trail brings you as deep into the bay as you can go without getting your feet wet. (Wear sneakers anyway, and bring insect repellent; mosquitoes flourish in the marsh pools.) The trail starts among white birches, short and stunted due to the bay's winter winds and salt. Beyond there, the path wends through hardwood groves, brightened with a ground cover of pink wild roses, bayberries, and goldenrod. Eventually the trail gives way to marshes at the peninsula's tip. The small inland ponds at the bay's edge are all that remains of a local effort to start oyster aquaculture decades ago. Marsh hay and wild grasses bend with the sea winds. Minnows streak in tidal pools, and razor clams exude streams of continuous

bubbles from their invisible burrows beneath the soggy sand.

A 58-site **campground** (902/831-2370; late June–early Sept.; $22–28) fronts the bay beneath tree canopies on a sheltered coastal notch. It offers a launderette, kitchen shelters, hot showers, Frisbee golf, a river beach, and nature programs.

€ Green Park Shipbuilding Museum and Yeo House

This heritage attraction (902/831-7947; early June–early Sept. daily 9 A.M.–5 P.M.; adult $5, child $2.50) lies on the edge of the provincial park. The Yeo House sits back on a sweep of verdant lawn. It's a gorgeous estate, fronted by a fence that rims the curving road. Inside, rooms are furnished with period antiques. Up four flights of stairs, the cupola—from which James Yeo would survey his shipyard—overlooks the grounds and sparkling Malpeque Bay. Behind the house, the museum has exhibits explaining the history and methods of wooden shipbuilding, Prince Edward Island's main industry in the 19th century. From these buildings, it's a short walk through a meadow to the water, where outdoor displays include a partially finished vessel cradled on a frame, plus historic shipbuilding equipment.

Bideford

The modest **PEI Shellfish Museum** (Rte. 166, 902/853-2181; late June–early Sept. Sun.–Fri. 10 A.M.–4 P.M.; adult $3, child $1.50) lies at the end of a red-clay road four kilometers north of Tyne Valley. Everything you could ever want to know about oysters and mussels is explained. A small aquarium contains mollusks, lobsters, snails, and inshore fish; outside, experimental farming methods are underway in the bay.

Lennox Island

A causeway off Route 163 brings you to this small island, home to 250 people of Mi'Kmaq ancestry intent on cultivating oysters, spearing eels, trapping, and hunting while pursuing recognition of the 18th-century treaties with England that entitled them to their land. The province's Mi'Kmaq are said to have been the first native Canadians converted to Christianity. Their history is kept alive at the **Mi'Kmaq Cultural Centre** (902/831-2702; summer Mon.–Sat.

10 A.M.–7 P.M., Sun. noon–6 P.M.). The 1895 **St. Anne's Roman Catholic Church,** a sacred tribute to their patron saint, grips the island's coastline and faces the sea. A crafts shop just north of the church markets Mi'Kmaq baskets, silver jewelry, pottery, and other wares.

Région Évangéline

The bilingual inhabitants of the Région Évangéline, the province's largest Acadian area, date their ancestry to France's earliest settlement efforts. The region offers French-flavored culture at more than a dozen villages spread west of Summerside between Route 2 and the strait seacoast. Miscouche, the commercial center, is a 10-minute drive west of Summerside on Route 2, and 30 minutes from the seaport along the coastal Route 11 is Mont-Carmel, the region's seaside social and tourist hub.

MISCOUCHE

As you approach from the east, the high double spires of **St. John the Baptist Church** announce from miles away that you've left Protestant, Anglo Prince Edward Island behind and are arriving in Catholic territory.

The village of 700 inhabitants at the intersection of Routes 2 and 12 began with French farmers from Port-la-Joye in the 1720s, augmented with Acadians who fled England's Acadian deportation in 1755. The settlement commands a major historical niche among Atlantic Canada's Acadian communities and was the site of the 1884 Acadian Convention, which adopted the French tricolor flag with the single gold star symbolizing Mary.

Musée Acadien

On the east side of town, Musée Acadien (Rte. 2, 902/436-2881; July–Aug. 9 A.M.–7 P.M.; adult $3.50) is geared as a genealogical resource center and also has exhibits of early photographs, papers, and artifacts, and a book corner (mainly in French) with volumes about

Acadian history and culture since 1720. Don't miss the documentary on events leading up to the 1755 Acadian deportation; it's screened on demand.

MONT-CARMEL

Two kilometers south of Miscouche and 24 kilometers west of Summerside, the backcountry Route 12 meets the coastal Route 11 (Lady Slipper Drive), which lopes south and west across Acadian farmlands to this hamlet, best

St. John the Baptist Church rises high above the town of Miscouche.

© ANDREW HEMPSTEAD

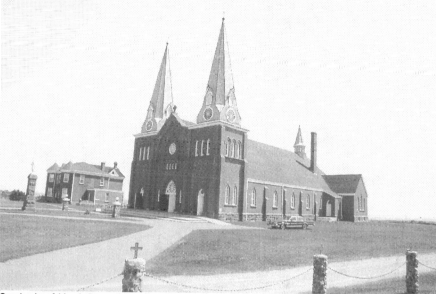

© ANDREW HEMPSTEAD

Our Lady of Mont-Carmel Acadian Church is an architectural highlight of Région Évangéline.

known for Le Village, a complex of lodgings with a restaurant. Mont-Carmel, 16 kilometers from Miscouche, makes a handy sightseeing base for touring the Région Évangéline.

◖ Our Lady of Mont-Carmel Acadian Church

This magnificent church, between Route 11 and the red cliffs fronting Northumberland Strait, reflects the cathedral style of France's Poitou region, which is renowned for its Romanesque churches featuring elaborate exteriors. The cathedral is open Sunday during Mass. For permission to enter at other times, ask at the **Musée Religieux** (902/854-2260; July–Aug. daily 1–5 P.M.), across the road.

CONTINUING ALONG ROUTE 11
Cap-Egmont

A few kilometers west of Mont-Carmel is the village of Cap-Egmont, best known for the very un-Acadian **Bottle Houses** (Rte. 11, 902/854-2987; early June–late Sept. daily 9 A.M.–6 P.M., July–Aug. 9 A.M.–8 P.M.; adult $4, senior

© ANDREW HEMPSTEAD

Cape Egmont Lighthouse is perched on red cliffs high above Northumberland Strait.

$3, child $1). They are the work of Edouard Arsenault, who in the 1970s mortared together 25,000 glass bottles of all colors, shapes, and sizes to form three astonishing buildings—a chapel with altar and pews, a tavern, and a six-gabled house. The structures qualified for inclusion in *Ripley's Believe It or Not*.

Turn off on the west side of the village to reach **Cape Egmont Lighthouse**. Although it's not open to the public, this light sits in a commanding position overlooking Northumberland Strait. Built in 1884, it is the same design as the one at Wood Islands (where the ferry from Nova Scotia docks), and like other lighthouses around the island it has been moved back from the ocean edge as erosion took its toll on surrounding cliffs.

Abram-Village

From Cap-Egmont, the scenic coastal Route 11 wends north for 10 kilometers and turns inland to this hamlet known for crafts. **La Co-op d'Artisanat d'Abram Village** (Abram's Village Handcraft Co-op), at the intersection of Routes 11 and 124 (902/854-2096; mid-June–mid-Sept. Mon.–Sat. 9 A.M.–6 P.M., Sun. 1–5 P.M.) is the area's definitive crafts source, with weavings, rugs, Acadian shirts, pottery, and dolls.

Western Prince County

Beyond Summerside and the Région Évangéline, Route 2 cuts into the interior out of sight of the seas. Nonetheless, most backcountry roads off the main route eventually finish at the water. To the west, the Northumberland Strait is the pussycat of summer seas, and the warm surf laps peacefully along the southern and western coastlines. The Gulf of St. Lawrence, however, is more temperamental, with a welter of rolling waves breaking onto the north shore.

For sightseeing information, stop at the provincial **Visitor Information Centre** in Portage (Rte. 2, 902/831-7930; July–Aug. daily 9 A.M.–7 P.M., June and Sept. daily 9 A.M.–4:30 P.M.), which is 43 kilometers north of Summerside.

MILL RIVER PROVINCIAL PARK

As you exit Route 2 at Woodstock, you enter a wooded realm on a ribbon of a road into Mill River Provincial Park. The park meshes lush landscapes with contemporary-style resort trappings and full recreation facilities, including the championship-quality Mill River Golf Course.

Recreation

Campers, resort guests, and day visitors all have access to the park's sports facilities. The eight tennis courts (lighted for night games) beside the hotel are free (but hotel guests have first dibs). At the campground, there's a marina with rentals (canoes and rowboats for $7 per hour and $28 per day).

The 18-hole, par-72 **Mill River Golf Course** (902/859-8873 or 800/377-8339) is generally regarded as one of Canada's top 50 courses and has hosted many national events through the years. The course spans 6,747 yards and is open May through October. During July and August, you'd be wise to make reservations 48 hours in advance. Greens fees range $50–60.

On warmer days, **Mill River Fun Park** (902/859-3915; July–early Sept. daily 11 A.M.–7 P.M.; $9 per person), is a good place for families looking for watery fun on waterslides and in outdoor pools.

Accommodations and Food

The three-story **Rodd Mill River** (Rte. 2, 902/859-3555 or 800/565-7633, www.roddhotelsandresorts.com; Jan.–Oct.; $130–275 s or d) is a sleek wood-sided hotel with 90 spacious and modern rooms and suites. Guests are attracted to the resort-style activities—golf, tennis, canoeing, swimming, and more—detailed in *Recreation*. The resort's **Hernewood Dining Room** boasts regionally renowned dining that draws an appreciative clientele from Summerside; expect a reasonably priced menu (from $16.50) featuring seafood specialties with a dish-of-the-day emphasis on salmon, halibut, or lobster (usually around $20).

The park's riverfront **campground** (902/859-8790; mid-June–late Sept.) has 72 sites: 18 unserviced ($22), 18 with two-way hookups ($25), and 36 with full hookups ($28). Amenities include kitchen shelters, hot showers, a launderette, and summer interpretive programs.

O'LEARY

On Prince Edward Island, O'Leary is synonymous with potatoes. Legend has it that the hamlet took its name from an Irish farmer who settled here in the 1830s. By 1872, rail service connected the hamlet with the rest of the island, and with that link in place, O'Leary was on its way to becoming Canada's largest potato producer.

O'Leary straddles backcountry Route 142, a five-minute drive from Route 2 and 50 minutes from Summerside. You might expect mountains of potatoes; rather, O'Leary (pop. 900) is a tidy place, nestled in the midst of surprisingly attractive fields of low-growing potato plants. If you're in the area during the autumn harvest, you'll see the fields lighted by tractor headlights as the farmers work late at night to harvest the valuable crop before the frost.

◖ Prince Edward Island Potato Museum

Don't be put off by the name; this museum (Parkview Dr. off Rte. 142, 902/859-2039; mid-May–mid-Oct. Mon.–Sat. 9 A.M.–5 P.M., Sun. 1–5 P.M.; adult $6, child $3) is an interesting stop that depicts the history of Prince Edward Island's most famous crop. The museum explains the story of the potato's humble beginnings in South America, the way the crop is grown and harvested, and how science has played a hand in the potatoes we eat today. A barn, a schoolhouse, and a chapel are out back.

WEST POINT AND VICINITY

Route 14 exits Route 2 at Carleton, eight kilometers west of Portage, doglegs west across the verdant farmlands, and heads to West Point at the island's western tip. From there, the scenic coastal route hugs the strait shore and brings some of the island's most magnificent sea views—a total distance of 80 kilometers to Tignish. Potato fields peter out at the strait coastline, which is definitely off the beaten tourist route. The coast's long stretches of beach are interspersed with craggy red cliffs.

Cedar Dunes Provincial Park fronts Northumberland Strait 30 kilometers from Route 2. It's only a small park, but it has

© ANDREW HEMPSTEAD

Cliffs fringe the west coast of Prince Edward Island, and in spots stairs lead down to narrow beaches where locals gather to swim and sunbathe.

a beach backed by sand dunes and a small campground (902/859-8785; late June–early Sept.) with 20 tent sites ($22) and another 39 two-way hookup sites ($25), a supervised beach, an activities program, a nature trail, kitchen shelters, a nearby campers' store, and hot showers.

West Point Lighthouse

Within Cedar Dunes Provincial Park is one-of-a-kind ❰ **West Point Lighthouse** (Cedar Dunes Park Rd., 902/859-3605, www.west-pointlighthouse.com; June–Sept.; $100–145 s or d), the only place in Canada where you can stay overnight in a lighthouse. There's just one guest room in the actual lighthouse ($145 s or d), but eight others are spread through adjacent buildings. The complex also has a small museum, a gift shop, and a dining room serving basic and well-priced seafood.

West Point to Miminegash

Beyond West Point, Route 14 cleaves to the coastline and heads north, first to **Cape Wolfe** (where British General James Wolfe is said to have stepped ashore on the way to battle the French in 1759) and then to **Howards Cove,** fronted with precipitous cliffs of burnished red. The distance from West Point to Miminegash is 36 kilometers.

MIMINEGASH

Nestled beside a body of water protected from the winds of Northumberland Strait by low dunes, Miminegash is renowned as the home of people who earn a living from collecting seaweed. Storm winds whip the sea on this side of the island into a frenzy, churning sea-floor plants into a webbed fabric that floats to the surface and washes to shore. This seaweed, known as **Irish moss,** is used commercially as a stabilizer in ice cream and other foods. It is harvested from the sea by boat, and also from along the shore—after a storm you may see workers raking the surf's edge, reaping the Irish moss and hauling it away with the help of draft horses. You

can learn about Irish moss farming at the **Irish Moss Interpretive Centre** (Rte. 152, 902/882-4313; early June–late Sept. daily 10 A.M.–7 P.M.; adult $3, child $1.50).

Part of the Irish Moss Interpretive Centre, the ❰ **Seaweed Pie Café** (Rte. 152, 902/882-4313; early June–late Sept. daily 10 A.M.–7 P.M.) serves light meals such as chowder and its namesake ($3.50 per slice).

ROUTE 12 NORTH TO TIGNISH

None of the three highways that lead north through Prince County to Tignish are particularly busy, but Route 12, along the Gulf of St. Lawrence, is the least traveled. It branches off Route 2 just beyond the village of Portage, 42 kilometers from Summerside.

Alberton

The seaport of Alberton (pop. 1,200) is the northern area's largest town. Named for Albert, Prince of Wales, the town began in 1820 with 40 families who worked at the shipyards in nearby Northport. Deep-sea fishing aficionados will readily find charter boats here. The **Alberton Museum** (457 Church St., 902/853-4048; June–Sept. Mon.–Sat. 10 A.M.–5:30 P.M., Sun. 1–5 P.M.; donation) is in a historic stone building that was originally a courthouse and jail. Exhibits delve into the town's history with antiques, clothing, and farm tools. The fox farming display is particularly interesting.

On the south side of Alberton, **Travellers Inn** (Rte. 12, 902/853-2215 or 800/268-7829; $85 s or d) has better-than-average motel trappings with 14 regular motel rooms and 13 kitchen-equipped units ($85–155), an indoor heated pool, a hot tub, and a pleasant atmosphere. The motel's restaurant serves basic beef and seafood dishes.

Jacques Cartier Provincial Park

It's only a short hop from Alberton back to Route 2, then 16 kilometers north to Tignish, but a worthwhile detour is to continue north on Route 12 to this coastal provincial park

(902/853-8632; late June–early Sept.), occupying the site where explorer Cartier is believed to have stepped ashore in 1534. The campground rims the gulf. It offers a supervised ocean beach, 23 unserviced campsites ($22), 30 sites with two-way hookups ($25), hot showers, a launderette, varied programs, and Frisbee golf.

TIGNISH AND VICINITY

Stories of legendary riches and the fur that created a haute-couture sensation almost a century ago embellish the lore of the remote northern peninsula. The world's first successful silver fox breeding began in the Tignish area in 1887. Charles Dalton—later knighted by the queen—was the innovator, and he joined with Robert Oulton from New Brunswick to breed the foxes. The pelts sold for thousands of dollars in fashion salons worldwide. From 1890 to 1912, the Dalton and Oulton partnership kept a keen eye on the venture and the number of silver fox breeding pairs. As luck would have it, generosity was their downfall: Their empire fell apart when one of the partners gave a pair of the breeding foxes to a relative. The cat—the fox, that is—was out of the bag. That single pair begat innumerable descendants that were sold worldwide, and breeding became an international business.

The area earned itself another major entry in national history when local fishermen organized Canada's first fishermen's union; the cooperative still processes and markets the bulk of the island's tuna. During summer, expect to see the "mossers"—Irish-moss harvesters clad in high rubber boots—in town.

Tignish (pop. 800) is simply laid out with Church Street/Route 2 as the main street. The town is 20 minutes from Alberton, a half hour from O'Leary, and 80 minutes from Summerside.

Sights

Make your first stop the **Tignish Cultural Centre** (Maple St., 902/882-1999; late

---

RAIL TO TRAIL

A joy for biking and hiking, the **Confederation Trail** spans Prince Edward Island, extending from Tignish in the west to Elmira in the east, a distance of 279 kilometers. Spur trails, including those leading to Charlottetown's downtown waterfront and the Confederation Bridge, add an additional 80 kilometers.

The trail was developed on a decommissioned rail line. The advantages of creating the trail on a rail line were twofold – there are no hilly sections, and the route passes through dozens of towns and villages. Add a base of finely crushed gravel, extensive signage, picnic tables, benches, and lookouts and you get one of the finest opportunities for outdoor recreation in all of Atlantic Canada.

The Confederation Trail is well promoted by both the provincial tourism authority and **Island Trails** (www.islandtrails.ca), a nonprofit organization that manages the system. Accommodations in villages along the route provide a handy base for traversing sections of the trail or as an overnight stop for those traveling longer distances. Some, such as **Trailside Inn** (Mount Stewart, 902/676-3130 or 888/704-6595, www.trailside.ca), have been specifically developed for trail travelers by offering beds and bike rentals.

May–early Sept. daily 8 A.M.–4 P.M.), which tells the natural and human history of the area, holds the usual array of tourism brochures, and offers public Internet access. Nearby, the **St. Simon and St. Jude Church** (902/882-2049; daily 8 A.M.–7 P.M.) is the town's stellar attraction, notable for its frescoes of the apostles and its mighty pipe organ. The organ, built by Louis Mitchell of Montréal, features 1,118 pipes from six inches to 16 feet in length. It was installed in 1882, and until the 1950s the organ was pumped by hand.

Accommodations

Right in town, an old red-brick convent has been converted to the **Tignish Heritage Inn** (Maple St., 902/882-2491; $80–110 s or d). The rooms are basic but adequate, and the inn has amenities such as a lounge area, laundry, and a kitchen, as well as a continental breakfast; it is a good place to spend the night before returning south.

North Cape

Some 16 kilometers north of Tignish, Route 12 ends at North Cape, the northern tip of Prince County. The dominant artificial feature, the **Atlantic Wind Test Site,** juts up from the windy plain with a federal project complex that tests and evaluates wind turbines. The adjacent **North Cape Interpretive Centre** (Rte. 12, 902/882-2746; July–Aug. daily 10 A.M.–8 P.M.; adult $3, senior and child $1.50) describes the science behind the wind turbines and also has a small aquarium.

Four kilometers before the cape, **Island's End Motel** (42 Doyle Rd., Sea Cow Pond, 902/882-3554, www.islandsendmotel.com; $65–95) overlooks the Gulf of St. Lawrence and is within walking distance of a beach. The most unique unit is a converted fishing boat, which has been dry-docked and renovated into a spacious and comfortable place to rest your head.

EASTERN PRINCE EDWARD ISLAND

The eastern third of Prince Edward Island, much of it within Kings County, is cut off geographically from the rest of the province by the Hillsborough River. One of this region's main attractions is the lack of crowds. It has none of the hype of Cavendish, and its activities and sights are more limited. If you're looking for sightseeing and recreation combined with natural attractions—coastal windswept peninsula beaches, seal colonies, sand dunes, and, inland, an improbable herd of provincial bison—you'll find that and more.

A two-lane highway circumnavigates the entire region, with farmlands laid out on the intensely red earth on one side, and the sea and sapphire blue sky on the other. The eastern shore, from Cardigan through to Murray Harbour, is tattered with little offshore islands and dozens of deeply indented bays and river estuaries. The region's southern climate is warm, humid, and almost tropical; islanders refer to this region as the "banana belt," and even such crops as wine grapes and tobacco thrive here. The long northern coast is nearly straight and uninterrupted, except at large St. Peter's Bay, where a tract of coast is protected as part of Prince Edward Island National Park. The northeast area is relatively remote, lightly populated and developed, and, inland, thickly wooded. As any islander will tell you, the county's northern portion is "far out"; i.e. far out of sight and out of mind from mainstream Prince Edward Island. The pastoral inland countryside is beautiful. It is cultivated in farms of corn, berries, grains, potatoes, and tobacco, and is rimmed on the north by forests and tracts of provincial woodlot plantations.

© ANDREW HEMPSTEAD

EASTERN PRINCE EDWARD

HIGHLIGHTS

◖ **Rossignol Estate Winery:** Unlike the typical wine country scenery, the vineyard at Rossignol is perched atop red cliffs high above Northumberland Strait – and the wine isn't bad either (page 58).

◖ **Seal-Watching:** Seal colonies inhabit islands along the southeast coast, but none are more accessible than near Montague (page 60).

◖ **Basin Head:** The unlikely combination of a fascinating fisheries museum and silica-filled

sand that "sings" as you walk across it makes for a stop that all ages will enjoy (page 63).

◖ **Prince Edward Island National Park, Greenwich Unit:** The Greenwich Unit of the island's only national park protects a moving sand dune system that is slowly burying a coastal forest (page 65).

◖ **Crowbush Cove:** Prince Edward Island is dotted with golf courses, but the best is the oceanfront Links at Crowbush Cove (page 66).

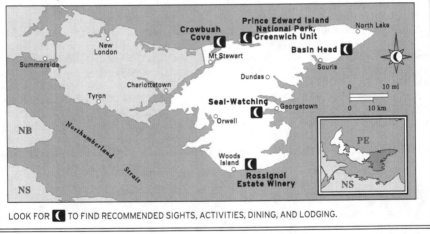

LOOK FOR ◖ TO FIND RECOMMENDED SIGHTS, ACTIVITIES, DINING, AND LODGING.

PLANNING YOUR TIME

Distances throughout the eastern portion of the island are much shorter than they may first appear when poring over the provincial road map. It is possible to drive around the entire region (under 400 kilometers) in one day from Charlottetown or to reach Souris, in the far eastern corner, in one hour from the capital. Visitors arriving on the island by ferry land at Wood Islands, from where most make a beeline for the capital, less than an hour's drive to the west, but this is a good starting point for exploring the region by heading in the opposite direction to Murray Harbour and beginning the convoluted coastal route

north and then west along the North Shore. Aside from exploring the provincial parks and admiring the coast-meets-farmland scenery, the three highlights of the drive are taking a **seal-watching trip** from Montague, visiting the museum at **Basin Head,** and admiring the wilderness of **Prince Edward Island National Park.**

Even though Prince Edward Island is tiny, the eastern portion of the province is well off the main tourist route. This means you will find well-priced accommodations. For this reason, it's a good place to take a break from touring. An ideal scenario would be to book a cabin for a couple of days and plan on

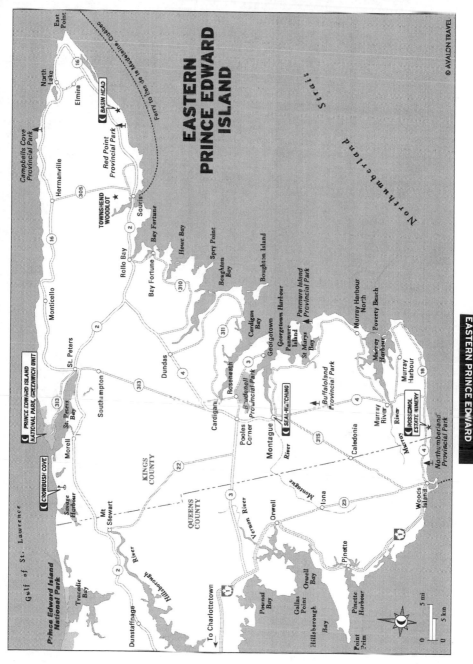

EASTERN PRINCE EDWARD ISLAND

spending time exploring the surrounding area, relaxing on the beach, strolling through the surrounding towns, golfing at one of the top-notch golf courses such as **Crowbush Cove,** or doing nothing at all. Larger villages have seafood markets, so plan on doing your own cooking, and then kick back in the evening with a glass of wine from **Rossignol Estate Winery,** which you pass right near the Wood Islands ferry terminal.

Along Northumberland Strait

The TransCanada Highway (Highway 1) extends east from Charlottetown for 62 kilometers to Wood Islands. This small village is the termination point for ferries from Nova Scotia, and also the starting point for touring through Kings County.

ORWELL

The small village of Orwell, 27 kilometers east of Charlottetown, has a couple of interesting historic attractions and is also the turn-off for those cutting across Kings County to Montague.

Sights

Orwell Corner Historic Village (Hwy. 1, 902/651-8515; June Mon.–Fri. 9 A.M.–4:30 P.M., July–Aug. daily 9:30 A.M.–5:30 P.M., Sept.–mid-Oct. Sun.–Thurs. 9 A.M.–5 P.M.; adult $7.50, child $3) is a restored Scottish village representing the 1890s. Buildings include the farmhouse, general store, dressmaker's shop, blacksmith's shop, church, and barns. In summer, there's a *ceilidh* (Celtic music and dancing) Wednesday at 8 P.M.

Off Highway 1 beyond the historical village is **Sir Andrew MacPhail Homestead** (Fletcher Rd., 902/651-2789; June–Oct. Sun.–Fri. 10 A.M.–6 P.M., Sat. 10 A.M.–8 P.M.), the summer home of a doctor of national renown who was involved in developing the island's potato industry. Three walking trails lead through the surrounding woods, and a restaurant is open daily (except Monday and Tuesday) for lunch and afternoon tea as well as weekends for dinner.

ORWELL TO WOOD ISLANDS
Lord Selkirk Provincial Park

Tucked on the eastern shore of Orwell Bay, an inlet off the larger Hillsborough Bay, is beachfront Lord Selkirk Provincial Park (902/659-7221; June–Sept.). The park, named for the Scottish leader of one of the early immigrant groups, is right off the TransCanada Highway, a stone's throw west of Eldon, 10 kilometers south of Orwell. Although the beach here isn't

Lord Selkirk Provincial Park

good for swimming, it's great for walking, beachcombing, and clam digging. The park's campground has unserviced sites ($22) and hookups ($25), a swimming pool, nine-hole golf course, mini-golf, laundry, kitchen shelters, fireplaces, and a nearby campers' store.

A naturalist program runs throughout summer, and the first weekend of August the park is the site of the annual **Highland Games,** which include piping, dancing competitions, Scottish athletic competitions, and lobster suppers. The park is open late June through early September.

Point Prim

Point Prim Lighthouse (902/659-2412; July–Aug.; free) is at the end of Route 209, which peels off the TransCanada Highway and runs 10 kilometers down the long slender peninsula jutting into Hillsborough Bay. It's Prince Edward Island's oldest lighthouse and Canada's only circular brick lighthouse tower. The view overlooking the strait from the octagonal lantern house at the top is gorgeous.

The **Chowder House** (Point Prim, 902/659-2023; mid-June–mid-Sept. daily 9 A.M.–8 P.M.) serves fresh local clams and mussels, chowder, sandwiches, and homemade breads and pastries.

WOOD ISLANDS

Not an archipelago of islands at all but a little village 62 kilometers east of the capital, this is where the ferry service from Nova Scotia unloads its cargo of vehicles and people.

Along the main highway through town is the **Plough the Waves Centre** (902/962-3761; mid-May–mid-Oct. daily 9 A.M.–6 P.M.), which holds the local information center and public Internet terminals.

Wood Islands Lighthouse

Ferry travelers will spot this traditional red-and-white lighthouse long before arriving at Wood Islands (stand on the starboard side for the best views). Dating to 1876, it is part of a small provincial park right beside the

Wood Islands Lighthouse is near the ferry dock.

© ANDREW HEMPSTEAD

ferry dock. You can climb to the top of the lighthouse (902/962-3110; June–early Sept. daily 9:30 A.M.–6 P.M.; free) and admire displays that tell the story of the ferry service and rum-running.

Accommodations

Meadow Lodge Motel (Hwy. 1, 2 km west of the ferry, 902/962-2022 or 800/461-2022; mid-May–Sept.) is a convenient accommodation if you're leaving the island early or arriving late. Standard motel rooms are $73–83 s or d, and a two-bedroom kitchen-equipped unit is $90.

Getting There

Between May and mid-December (the rest of the year, ice in Northumberland Strait restricts shipping) ferries depart Wood Islands 5–9 times daily for Caribou, Nova Scotia. The crossing takes 75 minutes, but expect to wait at least that long again during peak travel periods (July and August weekends). The round-trip fare is $61 per vehicle, including passengers. For a schedule, contact **Northumberland Ferries** (902/566-3838 or 877/635-7245, www.peiferry.com).

WOOD ISLANDS TO MURRAY HARBOUR

From Wood Islands, Route 4 continues into Kings County, making a sharp left inland to Murray River. Route 18 sticks to the coast, wrapping around Murray Head before leading into the town of Murray Harbour and then into Murray River.

Northumberland Provincial Park

Just three kilometers from Wood Islands, Northumberland Provincial Park (Rte. 4, 902/962-7418; late June–early Sept.) fronts the ocean, near enough to the terminal to see the ferries coming and going to Caribou. The park offers rental bikes, hayrides, a nature trail, a stream for fishing, an ocean beach with clam digging, and miniature golf. Facilities at the well-equipped campground include 60 sites (tent sites $22, hookups $25–28), a launderette, kitchen shelters, a nearby campers' store, and hot showers.

◖ Rossignol Estate Winery

Beyond the park, the highway crosses into Kings County and quickly reaches Prince Edward Island's only commercial winery (Rte. 4, 902/962-4193; May–Oct. Mon.–Sat. 10 A.M.–5 P.M., Sun. 1–5 P.M.). Try not to let the glorious ocean views distract you from the task at hand—tasting a wide range of reds and whites (including chardonnay and pinot cabernet), along with fruit wines and deliciously sweet blackberry mead. The winery produces 45,000 bottles annually and does everything right, including using oak barrels for aging. No tours are offered, but you are free to wander down the red dirt path leading to the ocean cliffs. The cellar door has tastings and sales.

Murray Harbour to Souris

From Wood Islands, you'll pass through tiny hamlets like Little Sands and White Sands, marked more by road signs than clusters of houses, as Route 18 approaches Murray Harbour. Enormous numbers of seals live in this well-sheltered harbor, and they love to loll about on offshore islands.

The Murray family settled the area and has namesakes everywhere: The Murray River flows into Murray Harbour, whose entrance is marked by Murray Head; seal colonies cluster on the harbor's Murray Islands; and the three seaport villages are Murray Harbour, Murray River, and Murray Harbour North.

MURRAY HARBOUR

On the south side of the bay is the small village of Murray Harbour. Beyond town to the east is **Beach Point Lighthouse,** from where seals are often visible.

Set on a five-hectare property, ◖ **Fox River**

Cottages (239 Machon Point Rd., 902/962-2881, www.foxriver.ca; May–Oct.; $775–925 per week July–Aug., $125–150 s or d nightly the rest of the season) offers four two-bedroom housekeeping cottages with screened porches overlooking the Fox River. Amenities include a canoe, rowboat, and laundry. Also in the area, **Harbour Motel** (Mill Rd., 902/962-3660, www.harbourmotelpei.com; $75 s or d) has seven kitchen-equipped units within walking distance of town.

Easily the best place to eat in town, **Brehauts Restaurant** (Rte. 18, 902/962-3141; Apr.–Oct. daily 8 A.M.–10 P.M.) has a big deck overlooking the river. The menu is strong on seafood, simply prepared and well priced.

MURRAY RIVER

The oval-shaped harbor is centered on the town of Murray River, hub of the island's southeast corner.

Sights

Children will love **King's Castle Provincial Park** (Rte. 348; mid-June–mid-Oct. daily 9 A.M.–9 P.M.) on the banks of the Murray River east of town. A grassy meadow is filled with concrete storybook characters, trails lead through the woods, and there's a riverside beach (complete with hot showers). A covered picnic shelter is the perfect spot for lunch.

If you like woodland walking, stretch your legs at **Murray River Pines,** a provincial woodlot near town. The site off Route 4 is remote. Look for an abandoned mill, the former provincial Northumberland Mill and Museum, now closed; the woodlot is inland behind the site. A 30-minute hike on the red-clay road leads to dense groves of red and white pines, abutted by stands of balsam, red maple, and red spruce. The largest pines date to the 1870s, when England's Royal Navy cut down most of the forest for masts. Somehow these trees survived, and they have become havens for birds of all kinds, including blue herons, kingfishers, swallows, blue jays, and chickadees.

Recreation

From the downtown wharf along Route 4, **Marine Adventures** (902/962-2494 or 800/496-2494; June–Sept.) operates a tour boat to the seal colonies of the Murray Islands. Along the way, you'll pass mussel farms and often spot seals and bald eagles. The trip costs adult $20, senior $15, child $12.

The **Old General Store** (Main St., 902/962-2459; July–Aug. Mon.–Sat. 9:30 A.M.–5:30 P.M., Sun. noon–5 P.M.; shorter hours in spring and fall) ranks as one of the island's best crafts sources and stocks folk art, linens, and domestic wares. It's open mid-June to mid-September.

Accommodations and Camping

On a small lake east of town, **Forest and Stream Cottages** (Rte. 18, 902/962-3537 or 800/227-9943, www.forestandstreamcottages.com; May–Oct.; $85–125 s or d) comprises six simple but tidy cottages, each with a kitchen, a bedroom, and a covered porch. Rowboats are supplied, and there's a playground.

Continue through town to the northeast to reach ◄ **Seal Cove Campground** (87 Mink River Rd., 902/962-2745, www.sealcovecampground.ca; June–Sept.), which overlooks offshore seal colonies. When you're done watching seals, there's a nine-hole golf course ($18 for a full-day greens fees), an outdoor pool, kayak rentals, and a playground to keep everyone busy. Tent sites are $28, hookups $35.

MURRAY RIVER TO MONTAGUE

Route 4 is the most direct road between Murray River and Montague, but Route 17 is more scenic.

Through the village of Murray Harbour North, **Poverty Beach,** at the end of a spur off Route 17, is a long narrow sandbar that separates the sea from the harbor. It's quiet, remote, and wrapped in a sense of primeval peacefulness. The peninsula is worth a trek, but think twice about swimming in the surf; powerful sea currents can be dangerous, and no lifeguards are around to rescue floundering bathers.

Panmure Island

Panmure Island, a remote and windswept wilderness, lies 15 kilometers north of Poverty Beach. It is linked to the mainland by a narrow strip of land, traversed by Route 347, which rambles out along the flag-shaped peninsula that wags between St. Marys Bay, Georgetown Harbour, and the sea. A supervised beach fronts the strait, and a wisp of a road angles into the interior and emerges at the waterfront with views of Georgetown across the harbor. Back on the mainland is **Panmure Island Provincial Park** (902/838-0066; late June–early Sept.). A campground here has 22 unserviced sites and 16 two-way hookup sites ($22–25), supervised ocean swimming off a beautiful white-sand beach, a launderette, a campers' canteen, fireplaces, and hot showers.

EASTERN PRINCE EDWARD

Buffaloland Provincial Park

Halfway between Murray River and Montague along Route 4, the 40-hectare Buffaloland Provincial Park (year-round; free) may seem deserted at first glance. If you look closely, though, you'll spot bison and white-tailed deer roaming the woodlands. The namesake herd began with 14 bison imported from Alberta in 1970 as part of a federal experiment to help preserve the almost-extinct species. There's still no population explosion, but the herd numbers 24 buffalo now. No guarantees, but mid-afternoon the bison herd often emerges to feed near the Route 4 fence.

MONTAGUE

Montague, 46 kilometers east of Charlottetown and 28 kilometers north of Wood Islands, is the largest town in Kings County, yet the population is under 2,000. The town is defined by the Main Street bridge over the Montague River. In fact, the town began as Montague Bridge in 1825, when the bridge was made of logs and the area had just four farms. Shipbuilding brought riches to the town, and many a schooner and other sailing craft was launched here on the broad river.

The town is uncomplicated, pretty, clean, and friendly. Everything important lies along Main Street, which slices through town and proceeds up, over, and down the bridge.

Sights and Recreation

GARDEN OF THE GULF MUSEUM

The Garden of the Gulf Museum (564 Main St., 902/838-2467; June–Sept. Mon.–Sat. 10 A.M.–5 P.M.; adult $3) is housed in an old post office overlooking Montague River at the bridge. The building is an impressive hulk of red brick with a steeply pitched roof, showing its French architectural influence. The collection includes exhibits on local history, including the colorful story of Trois Rivières, which was established nearby in 1732 by French entrepreneur Jean Pierre de Roma.

◀ SEAL-WATCHING

Cruise Manada (902/838-3444) leave from the town's marina on Route 4 or from the Brudenell

River resort wharf on Route 3. Both two-hour cruises sail 1–3 times daily. An onboard narrator provides information on local history and wildlife such as harbor seals, great blue herons, gulls, and ospreys. Tickets are adult $24, senior $22.50, children 5–13 $12.50.

Accommodations and Food

Overlooking the water, **Lanes Cottages** (33 Brook St., 902/838-2433 or 800/268-7532, www.lanescottages.com; $79–105 s or d) is a pleasant cluster of units with basic cooking facilities. Amenities include a playground and a Laundromat.

The deliberately rustic riverside **Lobster Shanty** (102 Main St., 902/838-2463 or 800/418-9430) has older motel rooms ($89 s or d) and chalets (from $169). The motel's riverview restaurant reigns as one of the region's best dining rooms, although it's a bit touristy.

Information

The junction of Routes 3 and 4, five kilometers north of Montague, is known as **Pooles Corner**. Here you find a provincial **Visitor Information Centre** (902/838-0670; June daily 9 A.M.–5 P.M., July–Aug. daily 9 A.M.–7 P.M.; Sept. 9 A.M.–4:30 P.M.).

BRUDENELL RIVER PROVINCIAL PARK

This 30-hectare park-cum-resort occupies a gorgeous pastoral setting on the peninsula that juts out into Cardigan Bay between the Brudenell and Cardigan Rivers. You enter the park from Route 3 three kilometers east of Pooles Corner, and the road winds through manicured grounds to the resort's main house and nearby chalets.

Recreation

Golfers enjoy walking the fairways of two golf courses (902/652-8965 or 800/377-8336; May–Oct.), Brudenell River and the newer Dundarave course, which plays to a challenging 7,300 yards from the back tees. The courses both rank among Atlantic Canada's superior golf greens and have been the site of various national and CPGA tournaments. Greens fees are $70 and $80 respectively.

Other park activities include canoeing ($35 a day), windsurfing ($45 for a partial day), horseback riding (902/652 2396; $28 for a one hour beach ride), indoor and outdoor pools, tennis, and boat tours. All park activities are open to campers, resort guests, and day visitors alike.

Accommodations and Food

The epicenter of the resort complex is **Rodd Brudenell River** (902/652-2332 or 800/565-7633, www.roddhotelsandresorts.com; May–Dec.; $140–260 s or d). Dating from the early 1990s, the resort holds three types of rooms: regular motel rooms in the main lodge; Countryside Cabins, which are simple free-standing units grouped together in strange configurations; and two-bedroom cottages with kitchens and fireplaces. Check the website for deals and packages. The resort's licensed **Stillwaters** is casually upscale and specializes in seafood entrées ($20–29); try the poached salmon awash in lemon sauce and, for dessert, shortbread squares topped with lemon meringue or the homemade parfait.

The modern units at █ **Brudenell Fairway Chalets** (Rte. 3, 902/652-2900 or 866/652-2900, www.fairwaychalets.com) are more like mini houses rather than chalets. Each has two or three bedrooms ($224 and $275 s or d, respectively), a well-designed kitchen, a lounge with TV, washing and drying facilities, and a deck with a barbecue. On the edge of the park, it's close to the golf course and also has its own pool and playground.

Campground

The park isn't all resort. Continue beyond the main entrance to reach **Brudenell River Provincial Park Campground** (902/583-2020; late June–late Sept.). Tent sites are spread through a wooded area ($22) while hookup sites ($25–30) have plenty of room to maneuver big rigs. Amenities include hot showers, kitchen shelters, a launderette, interpretive programs, a riverfront beach, and a walking trail that links the campground to the resort.

VICINITY OF BRUDENELL RIVER PARK
Georgetown

At the end of Route 3, beyond the park, Georgetown was once a major shipbuilding center. The naming of Georgetown was surveyor Samuel Holland's tribute to George III of England. The port boasted one of the island's most perfectly created deepwater harbors. Its early economy was built with British money, however, and when England's economy had a short-lived collapse, Georgetown lost its economic edge and never regained it. Georgetown slid into the shadows, replaced by Montague first as a shipbuilding and shipping center and then as the area's principal market town. It is now best known for the **King's Playhouse** (65 Grafton St., 902/652-2053; mid-July–mid-Sept.), a repertory company that stages dramas and comedies in a downtown theater year-round.

Cardigan

At this hamlet five kilometers north of the provincial park, the **lobster suppers** are well worth partaking in. You'll find them at the Olde Store (902/583-2020; late June–late Sept.; adult $26, child $16).

At the former railway station, **Cardigan Craft Centre** (902/583-2930; June–mid-Oct. Mon.–Sat. 10 A.M.–5:30 P.M.) is a reliable source of high-quality crafts, including handmade textiles, stained glass, and warm sweaters. Also in the station is a tearoom (Mon.–Sat. 10 A.M.–4 P.M.) serving inexpensive lunches.

BAY FORTUNE

Around 60 kilometers north of Cardigan along the Kings Byway, Fortune River flows into Bay Fortune, whose name originated long before the fortunes of Broadway fueled the local retreats of producer David Belasco and playwright Elmer Harris. Upriver six kilometers is the hamlet of Dingwells Mills, where *Johnny Belinda,* one of Harris's most successful Broadway plays and later a movie, was set.

Accommodations and Food

The **(◖ Inn at Bay Fortune** (Rte. 310, 902/687-3745 or 888/687-3745, www .innatbayfortune.com; late May–mid-Oct.; $150–325 s or d) has earned an international reputation thanks to the care lavished on the property by innkeeper David Wilmer. The estate was once the summer home of Elmer Harris, who designed the 19th-century version of a motel to house the entourage of thespians who traveled with the renowned playwright. The 18 guest rooms, 14 with fireplaces, are impeccably furnished and fill with natural light. The most sought-after is the two-level Tower Suite, which has sweeping water views from the upstairs lounge. Rates include a cooked breakfast.

A strong sense of conviviality pervades the inn's dining room, which is regarded as one of Canada's finest restaurants. Meals are served on the front enclosed porch during summer or inside with tables arranged before the fireplace when the weather is cooler. The creative menu features entrées emphasizing local produce from both the land and the sea (try scallops topped with strawberry and balsamic salsa), accompanied by a sophisticated wine list. Although you don't need to be a guest to dine here, many are, staying as part of a package (check the website).

Souris and Vicinity

Any islander will tell you that the fishing town of Souris is "far out," the end of the line on the beaten tourist track. The town (pop. 1,200), notched on the strait seacoast 80 kilometers east of Charlottetown and 44 kilometers north of Montague, garners unqualified raves for its setting. Consider Souris as a base for touring throughout the northeast. The location translates as good value for the dollar in lodgings and dining. The restaurants are plainly furnished and specialize in seafood platters, ranked by islanders among the province's best and freshest.

History

Unaware of the benevolent climate in the region's southern area, early French settlers from Port-la-Joye made their way up the Hillsborough River by 1724. Conditions were wretched. Plagues of field mice ravaged the fields and Souris village through the 1750s. Though the infestations eventually petered out, a reputation for rodents followed the seaport through the centuries and gave the village its name; *souris* is French for mouse. By 1800 the town emerged as a shipbuilding center and retained the role until the Great Age of Sail ended in the late 19th century. Simultaneously, canning as a method of preserving food developed as a seaport specialty, and for decades islanders stuffed lobster ad infinitum into cans for international export.

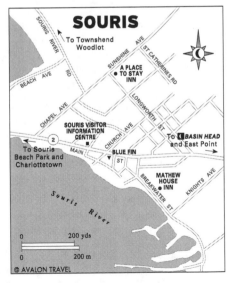

SIGHTS AND RECREATION

The town overlooks Northumberland Strait from sloping headlands, bounded in part by grasslands that sweep down to the water and in other parts by steeply pitched red cliffs. On the southern boundary, the Souris River rushes toward the sea with a gush of red-colored water and pours into the blue strait, like a palette of blended watercolor pigments.

Townshend Woodlot

Townshend Woodlot is a 106-hectare spread that closely resembles the island's original Acadian forest. In 1970 the International Biological Program designated the setting as one of the island's finest examples of old-growth hardwood groves. To get there, take Route 305 three kilometers north to the hamlet of Souris Line Road. The woodlot plantation lies off the road, fairly well hidden and obscurely marked—you may want to ask for directions in Souris. Acquired by the province in 1978, the woodlot lacks a clear hiking route, but it's easily walkable on a level grade of sandy loam. The groves meld beech trees—a species that once dominated half the island's forests—with yellow birch, red maple, and sugar maple, whose dark brown trunks stretch up as high as 32 meters. Eastern chipmunks nest in underground tunnels. Dwarf ginseng—rare on the island—and nodding trillium thrive.

❮ Basin Head

Formed by the winds, most sand dunes grow and creep along, albeit at a snail's pace. Basin Head's dunes are known as "walking" dunes for their windblown mobility. The high silica content of the sand here causes it to squeak audibly when crunched underfoot. Islanders poetically describe the phenomenon as "singing sands." The beaches at both Basin Head and adjacent Red Point Provincial Park are composed of singing sands. At Basin Head, the dunes are high and environmentally fragile; visitors should stay off the dunes and tread instead along the beach near the water's edge.

Behind the Basin Head dunes, **Basin Head Fisheries Museum** (Rte. 16, 902/357-7233; mid-June–late Sept. daily 9 A.M.–5 P.M.; adult $4, child $3.50) sits high on the headland overlooking an inlet. Here you'll find boats, nets, and a museum with expertly conceived exhibits detailing the historic inshore fishing industry and local coastal ecology. Behind the museum, a boardwalk leads across the dunes to the ocean.

Northeast of town, Basin Head is a popular destination for local cruise operators. Daytime sailings feature coastal bird-watching, and sunset cruises are timed to take in the colorful twilight. Cruises (usually around $30 per person) depart the Souris town wharf regularly, with all-day **lobster-fishing** expeditions offered in summer ($100 per person, with all gear supplied). Call the Souris Visitor Information Centre (902/687-7030) for a list of operators.

FESTIVALS AND EVENTS

The highlight of the event calendar is the **Souris Regatta** in mid-July, which features a sailing regatta, tub races, a midway, wood-carving demonstrations, and an arm-wrestling competition. That same weekend, musicians from across the island gather southeast of town at Rollo Bay for the **Prince Edward Island Bluegrass & Old Time Music Festival** (www .bluegrasspei.com).

ACCOMMODATIONS AND CAMPING
Under $50

As lodging prices are reasonable throughout the island, finding a place to stay for backpackers is less important than elsewhere in the region. That said, ❮ **A Place to Stay Inn** (9 Longworth St., 902/687-4626) is excellent in all regards. The downstairs of this large home within walking distance of town has been converted into a lodge, with separate male and female dorms, a kitchen, a living room with TV, bike rentals, a deck with a barbecue, and a laundry. Dorm beds are $20 per person.

$50-100

Guests at **A Place to Stay Inn** (9 Longworth St., 902/687-4626) may share the building with backpackers, but the two sections are completely separate. The upstairs guest rooms share bathrooms and breakfast is included in the rate of $65–70 s or d.

Fronting the ocean and within walking distance of a beach and Platter House Restaurant, **Lighthouse and Beach Motel** (Rte. 2, 902/687-2339 or 800/689-2339, www.lighthouseandbeachmotel.com; mid-June–mid-Sept.; $70–100 s or d) offers regular motel rooms with a light breakfast included in the rates. An old lighthouse on the property is rented by the week ($700) and has a jetted tub, separate bedrooms, and a kitchen. This lodging is two kilometers west of town.

A further six kilometers west is **Rollo Bay Inn** (Rte. 2, 902/687-3550 or 877/687-3550; $89–99 s or d). This lodging combines a re-created Georgian setting with 15 rooms, housekeeping units, and suites on spacious grounds with a licensed restaurant serving basic island cuisine.

$100-150

The lovely **Matthew House Inn** (15 Breakwater St., 902/687-3461, www.matthewhouseinn.com; late June–early Sept.; $110–175 s or d) sits on landscaped gardens within sight of the water. Built in 1885 by a local entrepreneur, its historic character has been preserved through meticulous restoration. My favorite of the guest rooms is Number 8, which has a soothing pastel-blue color scheme that blends perfectly with the polished hardwood floors and antique bed. Rates include a full breakfast.

Campground

Red Point Provincial Park (13 km east of Souris off Rte. 16, 902/357-2463; late June–early Sept.) has a campground with 32 tent sites ($22) and 58 powered sites ($28). Amenities include kitchen shelters, fireplaces, and hot showers.

FOOD

The ⟨ **Blue Fin** (10 Federal Ave., 902/687-3271; daily 8 A.M.–8 P.M.) is partly protected from the tourist crowd by its tucked-away location off the main street. But for well-priced simple seafood dishes, it's well worth searching out. The seafood chowder ($7) and the fish-and-chips ($10) are both excellent.

INFORMATION

Souris Visitor Information Centre (95 Main St., 902/687-7030; June–Oct. daily 9 A.M.–5 P.M.) is in a historic building in the middle of town.

North Shore

If you like photogenic landscapes, windy seacoasts washed with tossing surf, and weathered seaports, consider northeastern Kings County for a revealing glimpse of this seafaring island as it once was. Beyond Souris, the strait seacoast stretches 25 kilometers to windswept East Point, the island's easternmost point. On the equally remote gulf coast in this region, you'll find few tourists, a dozen tiny seaports, and a handful of lonesome lighthouses that stand as sentinels along the 75-kilometer-long coastline, strewn with centuries of shipwrecks.

FAR EAST
East Point

At the northeastern tip of Prince Edward Island, 25 kilometers northeast of Souris, Northumberland Strait and the Gulf of St. Lawrence meet in a lathered flush of cresting seas, sometimes colored blue and often tinged with red from oxide-colored silt. Here stands the 20-meter-high octagonal tower of **East Point Lighthouse** (off Rte. 16, 902/357-2106; mid-June–Aug. daily 10 A.M.–6 P.M.; guided tours adult $3, senior $2, child $1), which is still in use. The first lighthouse at this spot was built in 1867, but erosion has forced subsequent structures to be moved farther back from the cliff edge.

Elmira

Elmira Railway Museum (Rte. 16A, 902/357-7234; mid-June–early Sept. daily 9 A.M. 5 P.M.; $2) is the end of the line. Literally. This is where a rail line that once spanned Prince Edward Island came to an end. The original station now serves as the unspoken testament to the island railroad's halcyon years, with the province's only exhibits and documentation on rail service. It also holds a small gift shop and café, and has bike rentals. The bikes are for use on the **Confederation Trail,** the old rail bed, which has been converted to a walking and bike path that extends 279 kilometers to the other end of the island.

North Lake and Vicinity

North Lake harbor is one of four departure points for deep-sea fishing; anglers try for trophy catches of bluefin tuna. Expect to pay $20–30 per person for a three- to four-hour trip or about $400 for an eight-hour charter with four aboard. Trips depart daily during the July to mid-September season from North Lake, Naufrage, Launching, and Red Head harbors. **North Lake Tuna Charters** (902/357-2055), at North Lake harbor, is among the best.

Bluefin Motel (Rte. 16, 902/357-2053; July–Sept.; $70 s or d) caters to anglers with 10 basic rooms and a beach with clam digging.

Campbells Cove Provincial Park (Rte. 16, 5 km west of Elmira, 902/357-3080; late June–early Sept.) fronts the gulf with a beach, hot showers, kitchen shelters, and 48 serviced and unserviced sites ($22–28).

GULF SHORE
St. Peters

If you're in the area in late July or early August, check out the port's five-day **Blueberry Festival,** an islander favorite with concerts, entertainment, blueberry dishes, lobster and beef barbecue, and a pancake brunch.

St. Peters Park (Rte. 2, 902/961-2786;

ÎLES DE LA MADELEINE

Souris is the departure point for ferries to Québec's Îles de la Madeleine (Magdalen Islands), in the Gulf of St. Lawrence, 105 kilometers from the northern tip of Prince Edward Island and 215 kilometers from the closest point of Québec. This remote archipelago comprises 12 islands, six of which are linked by rolling sand dunes, and totals 200 square kilometers. The islands are renowned as a remote wilderness destination, featuring great beaches and abundant bird life. Villages dot the islands, and each has basic tourist services.

CTMA Ferry (418/986-3278 or 888/986-3278, www.ctma.ca) operates the MV *Madeleine* car/passenger ferry between Souris and the islands April through January. The 134-kilometer crossing takes five hours, with a schedule that includes 6-8 sailings weekly in each direction. Most runs leave Souris at 2 P.M. and leave Cap-aux-Meules for the return at 8 A.M. One-way passenger fares are adult $44, senior $36, child $22, vehicle from $82.

For information on the Magdalens, contact the local **tourism office** (128 Chemin Débarcadère, Cap-aux-Meules, 418/986-2245). This office also maintains an excellent website, www.ilesdelamadeleine.com, with detailed island information and links to accommodations.

EASTERN PRINCE EDWARD

mid-June–Sept.; $22–28 per night) has a campground with a choice of 11 unserviced sites and more than 70 full-hookup sites. Amenities include a launderette, kitchen shelters, free firewood, two swimming pools, mini-golf, and hot showers.

◖ Prince Edward Island National Park, Greenwich Unit

This national park has three units. (For the other two, see *Charlottetown to Cavendish* and *Cavendish* in the *Charlottetown and Queens*

County chapter.) Known as the Greenwich Unit, this six-square-kilometer tract of land encompasses a fragile dune system and wetlands, with a 4.5-kilometer trail leading over the dunes. Wind is slowly pushing the dunes back into the forest, burying trees that over time become bleached skeletons—an intriguing and unique sight. At the end of the road is **Greenwich Interpretation Centre** (902/963-2391; July–mid-Aug. daily 9 A.M.–8 P.M., June and mid-Aug.–Oct. daily 9 A.M.–5 P.M.). Admission to the park is adult $8, senior $7, child $4. To get there, take Route 313 west from St. Peters along the north side of St. Peters Bay.

MORELL AND VICINITY

Berries are the focus at Morell, 40 minutes from Charlottetown. The St. Peters Bay seaport makes much of the harvest at mid-July's six-day **Strawberry Festival,** with a parade, concerts, dances, barbecues, strawberry desserts, and other community events.

❰ Crowbush Cove

Along the coast just west of Morell is **Links at Crowbush Cove** (902/368-5761; May–Oct.), a highly acclaimed, 18-hole, par-73 golf course. A true links course in the Scottish tradition, Crowbush challenges players with 9 water holes and 8 holes surrounded by dunes. Greens fees are $80–100. Overlooking the golf course is **❰ Rodd Crowbush Golf & Beach Resort** (902/961-5600, www.roddhotelsandresorts.com; mid-May–mid-Oct.), comprising contemporary rooms in the main lodge and 32 two-bedroom cottages spread along the course.

Amenities include spa services, a fitness center, an indoor pool, tennis courts, and a restaurant overlooking the ocean. Most guests stay as part of golf packages, from $220 per person per night.

MOUNT STEWART

Located on the Hillsborough River, 35 kilometers northeast of Charlottetown, Mount Stewart grew as a shipbuilding center in the second half of the 19th century. Today, instead of shipyards, the draw is the **Confederation Trail,** a rail bed that has been converted to a hiking and biking trail that spans the entire island. Mount Stewart is a good place to base yourself for a day or overnight trip along a short section of the trail.

The main attraction in town is the **Hillsborough River Eco-Centre** (104 Main St., 902/676-2050; July–Aug. daily 10 A.M.–6 P.M.; free), which has displays on the river and its ecosystem, public Internet access, and a gift shop. Make sure to climb the tower out back for sweeping views up and down Prince Edward Island's major river.

The ❰ **Trailside Inn** (109 Main St., 902/676-3130 or 888/704-6595, www.trailside.ca; mid-June–late Sept.; $75 s or d) is named for the Confederation Trail, which passes through town. In a restored general store, the four rooms each have private bathrooms, hardwood floors, and televisions. For those looking at traveling the trail, this is a handy place to rent bikes ($25 the first day plus $10 per additional day). The in-house café (Fri.–Sun. from 4 P.M.) serves hearty country-style cooking and often hosts local musicians.

www.moon.com

DESTINATIONS | ACTIVITIES | BLOGS | MAPS | BOOKS

MOON.COM is ready to help plan your next trip! Filled with fresh trip ideas and strategies, author interviews, informative travel blogs, a detailed map library, and descriptions of all the Moon guidebooks, Moon.com is all you need to get out and explore the world—or even places in your own backyard. While at Moon.com, sign up for our monthly e-newsletter for updates on new releases, travel tips, and expert advice from our on-the-go Moon authors. As always, when you travel with Moon, expect an experience that is uncommon and truly unique.

MOON IS ON FACEBOOK—BECOME A FAN!
JOIN THE MOON PHOTO GROUP ON FLICKR

MAP SYMBOLS

▦ Expressway		🄲 Highlight		✕ Airfield		↧ Golf Course
⋯ Primary Road		○ City/Town		✈ Airport		🄿 Parking Area
━ Secondary Road		◉ State Capital		▲ Mountain		◢ Archaeological Site
▱▱▱ Unpaved Road		❀ National Capital		✚ Unique Natural Feature		▮ Church
▬ ▬ ▬ Trail		★ Point of Interest				▣ Gas Station
⋯⋯ Ferry		• Accommodation		⌇ Waterfall		⬭ Glacier
▰▰▰ Railroad		▼ Restaurant/Bar		▲ Park		▨ Mangrove
▦ Pedestrian Walkway		▪ Other Location		🄃 Trailhead		▨ Reef
▥ Stairs		Λ Campground		�skiing Skiing Area		▱ Swamp

CONVERSION TABLES

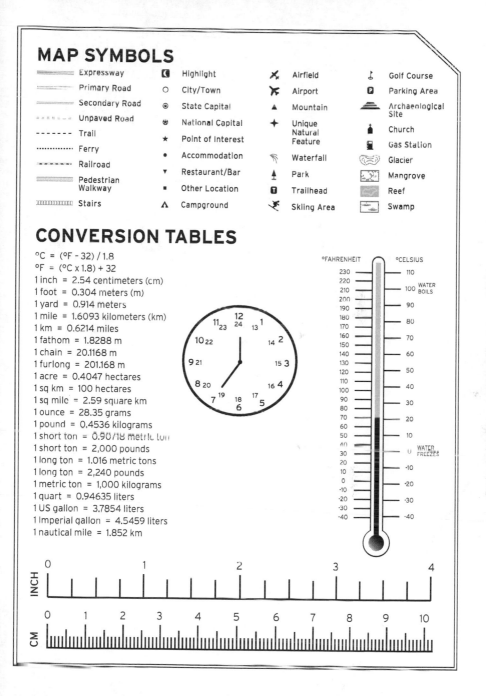

°C = (°F - 32) / 1.8
°F = (°C x 1.8) + 32
1 inch = 2.54 centimeters (cm)
1 foot = 0.304 meters (m)
1 yard = 0.914 meters
1 mile = 1.6093 kilometers (km)
1 km = 0.6214 miles
1 fathom = 1.8288 m
1 chain = 20.1168 m
1 furlong = 201.168 m
1 acre = 0.4047 hectares
1 sq km = 100 hectares
1 sq mile = 2.59 square km
1 ounce = 28.35 grams
1 pound = 0.4536 kilograms
1 short ton = 0.90718 metric ton
1 short ton = 2,000 pounds
1 long ton = 1.016 metric tons
1 long ton = 2,240 pounds
1 metric ton = 1,000 kilograms
1 quart = 0.94635 liters
1 US gallon = 3.7854 liters
1 Imperial gallon = 4.5459 liters
1 nautical mile = 1.852 km

MOON PRINCE EDWARD ISLAND
Avalon Travel
a member of the Perseus Books Group
1700 Fourth Street
Berkeley, CA 94710, USA
www.moon.com

Editor: Erin Raber
Series Manager: Kathryn Ettinger
Copy Editor: Christopher Church
Graphics and Production Coordinator: Lucie Ericksen
Cover Designer: Nicole Schultz
Map Editor: Albert Angulo
Cartography Director: Mike Morgenfeld
Cartographers: Kat Bennett, John Twena,
    Chris Markiewicz, Suzanne Service

ISBN-13: 978-1-59880-559-8

Text © 2009 by Andrew Hempstead.
Maps © 2009 by Avalon Travel.
All rights reserved.

ABOUT THE AUTHOR

© DIANNE MELTON

Andrew Hempstead

On his first trip to Atlantic Canada, Andrew Hempstead made a beeline for the coast to photograph the sunrise. He then headed to the nearest local restaurant, and wearily ordered the daily breakfast special without bothering to check what it was: cod fried in pork fat, pickled beets, and a side of baked beans.

With this traditional (and unexpected) introduction to Canada's east coast, Andrew set off on a road trip that stretched the term "unlimited mileage" on his rental car to the limit. Teaming up with knowledgeable local Ted Vautour for part of the trip, Andrew traveled to the farthest corners of all four provinces.

Andrew has been writing since the late 1980s, when, after leaving a career in advertising, he took off for Alaska, linking up with veteran travel writer Deke Castleman to help research and update the fourth edition of the Moon Handbook to Alaska and the Yukon. He has authored guidebooks to the Maritimes, Newfoundland and Labrador, Alberta, British Columbia, the Canadian Rockies, Vancouver and Victoria, and Western Canada, as well as contributing to guidebooks on the San Juan Islands and the Pacific Northwest. He has also worked on multiple guidebooks to New Zealand and Australia.

Andrew lives with his wife Dianne, daughter Brio, and two dogs in Banff, Alberta. When not working on his books, Andrew spends as much time as possible enjoying the wonderful surroundings in which he lives, hiking, fishing, golfing, camping, and skiing.